SCENARIO PLANNING

A Field Guide to the Future

Woody Wade

Designed by Nathalie Wagner, NaWa design

WILEY

John Wiley & Sons, Inc.

Library of Congress Cataloging-in-Publication Data:

Wade, Woody.
Scenario planning : a field guide to the future / Woody Wade.
    pages cm
Includes index.
ISBN 978-1-118-17015-1 (pbk)
ISBN 978-1-118-22692-6 (ebk)
ISBN 978-1-118-23741-0 (ebk)
ISBN 978-1-118-26444-7 (ebk)
1. Business forecasting. 2. Strategic planning. I. Title.
HD30.27.W336 2012
658.4'01--dc23
                                2011045563
Printed in the United States of America
SKY10020881_090220

To my beacons, Malcolm and Claire

Thanks

Like most endeavors, this book became a reality only because many people helped out, providing interesting perspectives and making valuable suggestions, not to mention prodding, pushing, and pulling. For being such enthusiastic sources of ideas and inspiration, I'd like to thank them here.

Nathalie Wagner designed the book beautifully, in the process dealing with a lot of silly questions and suggestions from a nondesigner like myself—and always with a smile. Her patience was angelic. As a collaborator on many previous writing projects, my brother Stuart Wade has been editing me in one way or another for years, and he looked over much of the text in faraway Austin, making dozens of useful suggestions for a nip here and a tuck there. Even farther away, in Mexico City, Christian and Kristine Arroyo helped me launch the web site 11changes.com, which got the whole ball rolling. I spent many a Sunday evening Skyping with them, and I'm grateful for all their good ideas and advice. (I'm also grateful for Skype itself.)

I'd particularly like to thank the four people whose work formed the basis of the case studies described in the book. These executives shared extensive information with me about the scenario planning exercises they undertook, and I'd like to express my sincere appreciation to them for their time and generosity, and their willingness to walk me through the results of their four quite different processes:

- Wilson Fyffe at Amblios in Singapore, whose company worked with the National Industries Corporation of the government of a beautiful (but unfortunately, unnamed) tropical archipelago and should therefore win some kind of prize for the best workshop location of all time.

- Larry Kilburn of the World Association of Newspapers in Paris, which brought in Stockholm-based Kairos Future to look at the future of that rapidly changing industry.

- Riikka Rajalahti at the World Bank in Washington, D.C., who called in one of the godfathers of scenario planning, Kees van der Heijden, to work with the bank and the government of India to explore how the country, and particularly its agricultural sector, might develop over the next 30 years.

- Ian Yeoman, now of Victoria University in Wellington, New Zealand, one of the world's leading experts on tourism development, whose work with VisitScotland was so amazingly thorough and imaginative.

Encouragement is also something every writer needs and cherishes. I was very lucky in this department, receiving moral support from many people here in Switzerland, including Nanci Govinder, Paul Lemeer, Mick Dawidowicz, Marc-Olivier Gemmet, Cory Ann Notari, Marnix Coopman, John Hurst, Olivier Taverney, and especially my terrific friends and mentors Chris and Christina Norton, whom I look up to every day.

Last, how could I not thank my two biggest cheerleaders, my kids Malcolm and Claire Wade? They kept me going throughout the project, and still do.

What's in this book?

CHAPTER 4 BLACK SWANS 140

History turns on events that are extremely rare yet have huge consequences. The same is probably true of your company's future.

CHAPTER 5 ARE YOU READY? 156

Most books about the future are full of predictions. "Just you watch: This will happen." This book isn't. Instead, it poses some questions about what *could* happen.

POSTSCRIPT THINKING THE UNTHINKABLE 186

A failure of imagination can have tragic results.

"The problem with the future is that it is **different**.
If you are unable to think differently,
the future will always arrive as a **surprise**.**"**

Gary Hamel

INTRODUCTION

Albert Einstein: World's Worst CEO?

A few days before Christmas 1930, Albert Einstein, the most celebrated scientist on earth, was sailing from Europe to New York aboard a luxury ocean liner. A lucky journalist who happened to be on board asked the physicist for an interview and was surprised that Einstein agreed.

Like today, the world was an uncertain place on the cusp of the 1930s—much more so, in fact. A worldwide Depression had begun, Fascists and Nazis lurked in dark alleyways all across Europe, and the prospect of another world war was very real. Holding Einstein in great esteem as an intelligent man—a genius, a visionary—the reporter opened his notebook and asked him a simple and by all means reasonable question: "Professor, what are your expectations for the future?"

Einstein's reply was surprising. No, not merely surprising—from such a man, his answer was astonishingly idiotic: "The future?" said Einstein,

"Oh, I never think about the future.
It will be here soon enough."

Huh? Imagine the CEO of your company saying that to the board of directors. How long would he last in his job? Or, never mind the CEO, imagine yourself saying this in a discussion with your boss: Her: "How do the three-year projections look, Quigley?" You: "Sorry, you talkin' to me, boss lady? Hey, I never think about the future. It'll get here on its own, believe me. Que sera sera!

Quigley, take some friendly advice: Update your resume.

As for Einstein, well, we're at the very beginning of this book, and who wants to start off on a negative note? So let's be charitable. Perhaps Einstein's "Don't worry, be happy" moment was nothing more than a reflection of what the French call a *déformation professionnelle*—the natural bias you develop thanks to the one-sided perspective you're exposed to in your work. Maybe the natural bias of scientists is not to focus on tomorrow but rather to concentrate on the here and now. For them, the salient question is, "What are the facts?" (i.e. the facts as they exist right now). Do the experimental results confirm my hypothesis? (That's today's experiment we're talking about.) How does the data look? (Not, mind you, how do you think the data might turn out to look five or ten years from now?)

So, we'll give Albert a break. It's not really his fault if his thinking was a little slipshod. After all, he was merely a nuclear physicist, not a manager, and if you keep this deficiency in mind, his *laissez-faire* attitude toward the future can perhaps be forgiven.

In a job interview, however, Einstein's "who-cares-let's-wait-and-see" mind-set regarding the future wouldn't land him many offers. It's simply inconceivable that a business leader—someone intelligent, someone expected to assume significant responsibilities—could ever think like this (and hope to be promoted).

That's because management, unlike science, is *entirely future-oriented*.

As a manager, most of the decisions you make today—and all of the really big ones—have to do with improving the chances for your organization to perform well in the future. Right now, based on the best information you have (which, by the way, isn't likely to be as reliable as experimental data produced under ideal laboratory conditions), you must make decisions about:

- How to grow your profits. . . *in the future*
- How to increase your market share. . . *in the future*
- How to position your new products successfully. . . *for the future*

- How to allocate your resources. . . *for the future*
- How to find new talent and integrate it into your organization. . . *for the future*
- How to improve your customers' satisfaction so they'll be loyal. . . *in the future*

. . . and countless other aspects of your business that will affect how competitive you will be—in the future. In fact, it's no exaggeration to say: Managers live for the future.

That's why you must give some thought to what the future will be like, because that's where you will live. It's not only here, in today's environment, where you have to be a winner, but in order to succeed over the long run, you'll have to compete in the world as it will exist in the future. What will this world be like? Nobody knows. But since it is going to be your operating environment, you'd better give it some thought!

When you do, don't limit your thinking to only the future of your company and its products. Look beyond your front door, and think about how your entire business environment—the whole world, even—will evolve. Visualize how the future could unfold and create a new and different business "landscape" compared to the world that you're operating in today.

In this as-yet-unknown future landscape, your company will have to be competitive.

In this new landscape, the terrain may differ greatly from what you're used to today. What's more, it won't be only the background scenery—the economic and social settings, the technologies, politics, and regulations that underpin your day-to-day existence—that will evolve between now and then. It's highly likely that different competitors will roam that landscape with you, as will different suppliers, not to mention a whole new set of people with new attitudes and expectations, many of whom today are still youngsters, their tastes and preferences and desires not yet fully formed. These are the people you'll need to sell to, hire, and inspire if you're going to thrive 10 years down the road.

The earlier you can sharpen your vision of the road ahead, identifying and describing the changes you'll likely be dealing with, the better prepared you'll be for the new competitive challenges and opportunities this landscape will have to offer you.

But (I hear you saying) nobody knows how the future is going to turn out! How can you describe something that's not yet here to see?

That's what this book is all about. It will introduce you to a planning method that can open your eyes to future changes and opportunities that might materialize, help you maximize your flexibility so you can compete effectively in different landscapes that may emerge, and prepare you not just for the future, but for several possible futures.

There's no better time to start this process than now. After all, as Einstein said, "The future will be here soon enough." And he was the world's smartest guy.

$$U = Mgh = Mgl\sin\alpha \qquad \frac{d\omega}{d\psi} = -\frac{1}{v^2}\frac{dr}{d\psi} \qquad \frac{d^2\omega}{d\psi^2} = \frac{1}{v^2}\frac{d^2 b}{d\psi^2}, \frac{2}{v^3}$$

$$k = \frac{1}{2}Mv^2 + \frac{1}{2}I\omega^2$$

$$-M\omega^2 + \frac{1}{2}J\left(\frac{v}{R}\right)^2 = \frac{1}{2}Mv^2 + \frac{1}{2}\cdot\frac{2}{3}Mv^2 \qquad \frac{d^2 r}{dl^2} = -\frac{1}{v^2}\left(\frac{J}{\mu}\right)^2\frac{d^2\omega}{d\varphi} \Rightarrow \frac{d^2\omega}{d\varphi^2} + \omega =$$

$$\vec{S} = \vec{N} \Rightarrow \left(\frac{dJ}{dt}\right)_3 = \frac{dJ}{dt} + \vec{\omega} \wedge \vec{S}$$

$$t = 0 \qquad k = \frac{1}{2}M\dot{x}^2 = \frac{1}{2}M[\omega_0 A\cos\omega t$$

$$\vec{S} = \vec{N} \qquad \Omega = \frac{I_3 - I_1}{I_1}\omega_1 \qquad \theta = \theta_0 \qquad \langle K \rangle = \frac{\int_0^T k\,dt}{t_0} = \frac{1}{4}M\omega^2 A^2$$

$$\vec{\omega}\wedge\vec{S} = \vec{N} \qquad \vec{F} = \frac{C}{v^2}\vec{r} \qquad F = -\frac{dU}{dv} = \frac{C}{v^2}$$

$$\frac{C}{r^2} \Rightarrow \vec{F} = \frac{C}{v^2} \qquad \frac{\omega_0}{2\pi}\int_0^{2\pi}\cos^2\omega_0 t\,dt = \frac{1}{2\pi}\int_0^{2\pi}\cos^2 y\,dy = \frac{1}{2}$$

$$U(r) = \frac{C}{vr} \qquad \frac{dU}{dr} \qquad x = A\sin\omega t \Rightarrow U = \frac{1}{2}C x^2 = \frac{1}{2}C$$

$$U(r) = \frac{C}{vr} \qquad \lambda \qquad s\frac{1}{v} \qquad \sin^2\omega t\,dt = \frac{1}{2} \qquad \frac{1}{2}M\omega^2 A^2$$

CHAPTER 1

ESCAPING THE TYRANNY OF THE PRESENT

Is This Any Way to Plan?

Most organizations do some kind of long-range planning. Yours probably does.

At many companies, though, in spite of all the time and personnel invested in planning, the actual strategic plan that emerges at the end of the process is based on—no, practically joined at the hip with—a set of forecasts that implicitly consider the future as an extrapolation of the present, a more or less linear continuation of the situation these companies are already in, right here, right now. Isn't that convenient?

The planners in your company might disagree. I'm sure they see their work as being a little more sophisticated than that. "Extrapolation? No way!" they will sputter. "Stop insulting us! We do a *lot* more than just taking known data points from the past and extending a straight tangent line beyond the present limit!" (I'm not sure if people actually talk like that, but this is more or less how they will defend themselves.)

PRETTY MUCH THE SAME

But that *is* what they're doing. Well, to be more precise, there are two kinds of extrapolations going on in most companies. The first is a *mathematical* operation. And here, I could sympathize with why planning experts might take umbrage at the idea that "extrapolation" is all they do, since any high school sophomore should be able to produce a decent projection in 10 minutes on an Excel spreadsheet: Just plug in the numbers from the last couple of years and you're done. *"Hey guys! I did the forecast! Hurry up and write the strategic plan so we can get back to Call of Duty!"*

This is not the image highly paid strategic planners want to project.

Despite their protests, mathematical extrapolation is the mechanical basis for most forecasting. To cover all the bases, planners may also come up with what they misleadingly call *scenarios*—separate forecasts representing the "most likely" set of variables, the "best" case, and the "worst" case. All this is achieved by increasing or decreasing some or all of the variables, running the numbers again, and seeing what pops out. Numbers down: worst case. Numbers up: best case. *It's easy!*

So, yes, this is all the product of extrapolation. But not just the mathematical kind. At the heart of this kind of planning, a second kind of extrapolation is at work here, and for lack of a better phrase, I'll call it *mental extrapolation*. What I mean by this is that the plans and strategies that emerge from the usual process are based on forecasts that are ultimately predicated on the idea that everything that will shape the future is represented by the variables in the model. Short and sweet: "We've got it all covered!"

No, they don't. What the planners don't see is that, in addition to tweaking the numbers, what they're really extrapolating is an entire mental image of how their business environment will evolve: "*As far as we're concerned,*" they're telling themselves, "*tomorrow will just be a variation of today. A bit more of this, a bit less of that, depending on how the variables change. It won't be exactly the same as today, but. . . pretty much.*"

With this mind-set, next month will be *pretty much* like this month, next year *pretty much* like this year, and 10 years from now *pretty much* like today. For them, as long as the forecasting model includes all the "right" variables, then the future can be only a few mathematical tweaks off of today.

This is flawed thinking. So flawed that it could have fatal consequences for any organization that relies too much on such forecasts.

Because no matter how sophisticated their forecasting model may be, the planners—by basing their view of the future exclusively on how the variables develop—are making an underlying assumption that, other than these variables, nothing much will change. They're saying that the risks and opportunities tomorrow will be similar to those they're dealing with today; only the magnitude will change. That's an egregious oversight.

DOOMED TO IRRELEVANCE

In a world where nothing much changes, this would probably be an acceptable way of forecasting the future. But here's the problem: *We don't live in that world*.

Exchange rates and raw material prices and market shares and hundreds of other variables may move up, down, or sideways, but no amount of manipulating these inputs will reveal to you that a new competitor may appear, a new technology may emerge, an entirely new market may be created (or an existing one wiped out), or a new type of customer may be developing. And *these* are the kinds of events and developments that are more likely to shape a company's future!

So, the strategic plans meticulously drawn up based on the notion of continuous, incremental, evolutionary, and ultimately rather predictable change are, well, perhaps not *totally* worthless, but doomed to irrelevance the moment something big and unforeseen in the business environment does change.

In fact, one of the few things you can say with certainty about plans drawn up this way is that the "most likely scenario" will never actually materialize! How comforting it is to have this forecast in the drawer! It creates such a wonderful sense of security. . . reassuring you. . . lulling you. . . zzzzzz.

I ask you: Is this any way to plan for the future?

Two thousand years ago, Cicero spoke of "the tyranny of the present," and there is hardly a more apt phrase to describe the mind-set that can lull even a highly intelligent executive into believing that the future will just be a variation on a theme—that theme being "today."

With projections in hand—best case, worst case, most likely case—it's easy for managers to delude themselves into thinking they can see the future they'll be competing in. And once they've tricked themselves into seeing the road to the future as a nice, straight line, it's not a big leap of faith to start believing they are in control of the way the future will turn out.

However, by basing their view of tomorrow on the lay of the land today, there's a good chance that they will also base important decisions on the assumption that they know how their future business environment will look, when in fact that environment may be radically different from their expectations—and not because the variables they projected evolved differently, but because entirely different factors came into play that they hadn't anticipated and hadn't even thought about.

Instead of developing in a nice straight line, the road to the future twists and turns. It's forked, bumpy, and full of potholes and unexpected dead ends. The guardrails are flimsy. And there are very few road signs to guide you. You have to navigate much of it without a map. To paraphrase the late, great Peter Drucker, predicting the future based on extrapolating from the present is like driving down this road at night while looking out the back window.

Instead, we need to figure out a way to see where the road ahead is leading. That way is called *scenario planning*.

Don't Forecast the Future—Anticipate It

If one of your tasks as a manager is to help ensure that your organization remains competitive 5 or even 10 years from today, then visualizing how the future may develop between now and then is not a meaningless parlor game; it's a vital necessity. You need to understand today how your company is likely to be challenged when, tomorrow, the competitive landscape around you changes—and change it will!

But if forecasting isn't the best way to visualize the future lay of the land, what is? Nobody has a crystal ball. Is there really a way to see what's ahead?

Yes and no.

No, because, well, as I said: Nobody has a crystal ball. You will never be able to see with absolute certainty today the one and only future that will materialize even next Tuesday, let alone 10 years from now.

Yes, because a methodology does exist that can help you visualize the future. Or to be more precise, it doesn't help you see *the* future, but *a range of alternative futures*. Each one of these futures, called *scenarios*, could plausibly emerge, depending on how developments that are going on today continue to unfold. None of the futures is guaranteed to come to pass, of course. And in fact, they are not likely to be very accurate, at least not in detail. But accuracy is not the objective. By creating several alternative visions that you believe have a reasonable chance of emerging, you are in a better position to prepare yourself and your organization for the flexibility you'll need to face whichever future does, in fact, unfold.

The method is called *scenario planning*, and it's a productive, creative, and even exciting way to develop the groundwork for a strategic plan that doesn't bet the company's future on the emergence of a single "most likely scenario" (i.e., one that's largely extrapolated from today's numbers).

Instead of relying on projections that basically paint a picture of your future business landscape as a variation on the way it currently looks, scenario planning challenges the very idea that there is *a* future that is "most likely" to emerge. Instead, it recognizes that at any point in time, there is not one *single* future that is certain to develop, but an array of possible futures that could potentially unfold. Which one actually does emerge depends on how trends that are happening all around us now play out, as well as on other potentially significant events and changes that might occur along the way.

The outcome of the scenario planning process is a portfolio of future scenarios, each representing a different way your business landscape could look in a few years, and not just the landscape, but also the players who inhabit it—your competitors, customers, suppliers, employees, and other stakeholders. The scenarios will naturally differ from each other in some key aspects, probably even dramatically so, but in its essential makeup, each one will be realistic and entirely possible, given your reading of today's trends. Based on these different scenarios, you and your planning team can then sit down and formulate more flexible strategies that ensure your organization has the agility to compete in whichever future does in fact come to pass—even one that is different again from the scenarios envisaged.

The key benefit of the process is therefore not that it reveals tomorrow's deep mysteries to you. Alas, the unknown will remain unknown. Rather, what scenario planning does do is open your eyes to different ways the future might (i.e., *could*) develop, and with these insights, you're more likely to make more flexible, more thoughtful, and *better* decisions today.

"But Our Projections Were Right!"

When Being Right Isn't Enough

It may be a tired cliché, but over time, constant change is about the only thing you can count on in your business landscape. Unfortunately, conventional forecasting gives you only a dim idea of how different the future environment may be that's in store for you. It can't capture the full extent of the changes that *could* take place—some of them monumental in terms of a company's future success. . . or failure.

With a few rare exceptions, when a company fails, it's not because it didn't project next year's interest rates accurately, or get the price of a barrel of oil right. More often, a company goes out of business because of its inability to visualize how fundamentally its competitive landscape would change for the worse if an unanticipated new technology were to arrive on the scene, if a new competitor were to appear, or a restrictive new regulation were to be put in place. Or the company simply didn't have the imagination to recognize changing market preferences—that is, needs that would be better fulfilled by someone else.

Taken by surprise, a firm in this situation usually tries to react, but sometimes it's just too late. The corporate graveyard is full of companies that were unprepared for changes in their business landscape, among them:

- **Polaroid.** For 50 years, the name Polaroid was synonymous with instant photography. The company declared bankruptcy in 2001, having failed to anticipate the advent of a new kind of photography—digital—that really *was* instant and didn't require that you shell out money for film.

- **Sun Microsystems.** Failed, you say? Sun was acquired by Oracle in 2010 for $7.4 billion, which doesn't sound like a failure. But that amount pales in comparison to its peak valuation of over $200 billion a few years earlier. Even though it was one of the great innovators during the IT boom of the 1980s and 1990s, Sun failed to adapt its strategy from a focus on hardware to one on software; as a result of its hardware fixation, in the words of one of its own executives, "We did not understand the economic disruptive force of either Intel or open source until it was too late."

- **Swissair.** For decades, Swissair was considered one of the world's best airlines. However, it was pursuing a cash-intensive strategy of snapping up smaller regional airlines in Europe when two factors came into play that the company hadn't foreseen. First was the launch of budget carrier EasyJet, which undercut Swissair's much more expensive fares and took passenger traffic away. Second were the terror attacks on September 11, 2001. Air travel was hit hard, and Swissair's profitability and cash flow, already weakened, suffered a catastrophic blow. Unable to make debt payments and unexpectedly cut off from additional funding by its largest bank (a third nasty surprise), the airline's fleet was grounded, and within six months the once-proud carrier went into liquidation.

- **Borders.** Once the pioneer of the "big-box" book-retailing concept, Borders closed its doors for good in 2011. The company wasn't able to adapt to two changes brought about by the Internet: competition from online booksellers and the rise of the e-book. "I'll miss them," said one customer, "but I'm not going to buy another paperback in my life. There's no reason anymore." Could Borders have adapted to this sea change in the way people read? We'll never know, although rival retailer Barnes & Noble seems to be managing all right for the time being.

- **Napster.** Napster may seem an odd example to include on such a list, since the company was essentially shut down by lawsuits aiming to stop the infamous peer-to-peer file sharing service from distributing copyrighted music illegally. But could there be a clearer case of management failing to foresee a critical change looming in its legal environment?

In the annals of corporate history, sadder words than these may be hard to imagine: "We didn't have a plan for X. And then X happened."

The last flight

It's a Leadership Issue

How can you lead if you can't see where you're heading?

As I noted in the Introduction, Albert Einstein didn't find it very compelling to waste his time worrying about the future. For him, it was the present, and all the knowledge that can be gleaned right now, that held more interest. Being a scientist, this was apparently his default way of looking at the world. The present matters. The future, Einstein must have thought, can wait.

This unfortunate Einsteinian attitude would make for a serious leadership shortcoming in a manager. In business, someone who thought this way wouldn't be able to lead his or her organization much further than the company cafeteria, to say nothing of leading that organization into the great unknown—the future. How can you make ambitious plans for your organization 5 or 10 years from now and convince your colleagues (not to mention your board) to support your vision, if your time horizon doesn't stretch beyond 6:00 p.m.?

Such a manager would forever be *reacting* to events instead of *anticipating* them. And that is the key skill you need as a business leader to maximize your company's chances of success over the long term: the ability to *anticipate the changes* that could emerge in your landscape tomorrow. Only with this understanding is it possible to confidently make the decisions that will help prepare your organization for the changes to come.

The essence of leadership, therefore, is to be constantly gaming the future—grasping its possibilities, communicating a vision of the role you want your organization to play in this new future landscape, and inspiring your team to help you make that vision a reality.

Scenario planning is therefore a critical tool for anyone who is not just managing, but also leading. It facilitates your ability to create a realistic vision for the future, as well as your ability to craft the strategies that will make you successful once you get there.

Scenarios ≠ Predictions!

Before we delve into scenario planning and how it works, it's important to dispel a potential misunderstanding.

Scenario planning doesn't try to predict an ironclad picture of how the future will turn out. Only Nostradamus could do that.

Instead, scenario planning aims to illuminate and explore different ways the future *might* realistically develop. The scenarios generated by this thinking (always more than one, as we'll see in a moment) should be regarded as insightful indicators of what *could* come to pass in the future, depending on the breaks.

The idea is that this mix of trends and developments will make a particular kind of future more likely. Scenarios are therefore stories that reveal how a certain future constellation of market and environmental factors would look and feel.

But alas, a scenario is not a prophecy that any particular future will actually come to pass. If only it were that easy!

By going through a scenario planning process, you're acknowledging that predicting "the" future is not possible and that instead, there are myriad forces, interacting and feeding off each other, that will be driving your organization toward some unknown future. Think about that. It's a humbling admission to make, not always an easy one for a Master of the Universe who is used to calling all the shots in his or her company. To get the most out of scenario planning, you have to let the shots call themselves!

That Newfangled* Thing? Why, It's Just a Flash in the Pan!

How can you analyze a market that doesn't exist? The answer: You can't. Which helps explain why many companies fail to recognize the potential threat of a disruptive new product that comes along, nibbling away at their market share while flying below the radar (to mix a metaphor). The newcomer may be selling only to fringe customers at that early stage of the game. If they notice the upstart at all, the big established companies talk themselves into believing that it's not a serious threat, but just a flash in the pan.

However, this flash in the pan may move from fringe customers to the mainstream and succeed in supplanting the big companies' products, eventually even forcing the big guys to launch their own me-too version of the newfangled product, just to remain competitive. But by then it may be too late to regain their market leadership.

Why do companies deceive themselves this way? Clayton Christensen explored this failing in his book *The Innovator's Dilemma*. In a nutshell, here's what he says happens:

- Established leaders use conventional market research tools and techniques to gather feedback from their major customers. "Are you interested in this new gadget? No? Whew!" All's well, then. The problem is that by studying the reaction of their best customers to the new product, they aren't really finding out about its potential, because it's precisely these customers who will be among the *last* to make the switch to something new and disruptive. In other words, don't always trust your own market research. If you do, you're screwed!

- While the leading companies are busy making decisions based on standard metrics such as market size and growth, the disruptive new products may manage to encroach into the market on such a small scale that, at first, they don't set off any alarm bells. Almost by definition, upstarts are elusive and unpredictable. Conventional measuring tools can miss them, or at least fail to recognize the impact they are starting to have.

- Big companies, for the most part, also tend to focus on big markets. They have to; that's where they have to go for growth and high returns. Disruptive innovations, on the other hand, may start out selling to a small, low-margin segment of the market—one that's not only less visible but less attractive as well. What's more, upstarts may be willing to forego profits until they've gained a toehold in the business. The big companies simply don't notice what's happening until the threat to their market share has actually materialized.

All this boils down to one thing: Even very good forecasts made today will never capture the eventual impact tomorrow of a small, disruptive innovation. But a company that questions what *could* happen *if* a disruptive new product enters its market will be in a better position to respond to one if and when the situation comes up.

Organizations need to ask themselves these what-if questions on a regular basis. Once again, scenario planning to the rescue!

*Insert your own choice of "newfangled thing" here: personal computer, cable TV, digital camera, DVD, e-book, iPod. . .

A BINARY FUTURE?

Imagine you're the CEO of a company that operates in an unusually simple environment: In this make-believe world, there is only one variable that is relevant to your ability to compete. Let's say this variable can become either red or yellow. If it's red, your company will be in great shape. But if it's yellow, you'll face an uphill struggle.

To make matters a little more interesting, imagine that for the moment, this red or yellow variable is a wishy-washy shade of orange, and you will know only one year from now whether the "red scenario" or the "yellow scenario" will prevail. One of them *will* prevail, however. You just don't know which one.

What kind of strategic plan would you formulate in this situation? If you're like most CEOs, you would recognize that it's very risky to bet the company's future on only one outcome. Instead, you would want to develop a strategy that maximizes your readiness for *either* red *or* yellow to emerge. This means devising a plan to assure you the flexibility and agility that you'll need to adapt quickly to whichever scenario actually materializes a year down the road.

In practice, what would this mean? Keeping your eyes open, making sure you're adept at recognizing when orange no longer looks quite so orange but is becoming a little more red or yellow than before, and having all the operational elements in place to take advantage of the favorable red scenario, if that's what happens, or to quickly put your defensive plan into action if the yellow scenario emerges instead.

In other words, you would not establish a plan based on projections of the current environment, but one based on the idea that the future could unfold in more than one way, resulting in alternative scenarios: a red one or a yellow one.

Let's look at what would happen if you did base your view of the future on projecting today's situation to tomorrow. Instead of arriving at two alternatives, red and yellow, your analysis of today's conditions would lead you to believe that what the future has in store is simply more orange.

However, we know (because we made up this example) that "orange-ness" is just a temporary condition. In reality, one of the two scenarios, red or yellow, is going to dominate. If your strategy is predicated on the future being orange, you are going to be poorly positioned if the red scenario materializes, and possibly just as poorly positioned if the yellow one does.

Your planning team may try to convince you that orange will be the most likely scenario to develop. Why wouldn't they? Life has been orange so far. But betting on things to stay orange will guarantee you a suboptimal outcome, because either outcome (red *or* yellow) will take you by surprise. The result: You'll be scrambling to get a more appropriate strategy in place rather than calmly implementing one that anticipated the possibilities.

Today, your only problem is that you don't know which scenario will materialize. That's not an ideal situation to be in, but it isn't the end of the world. It just means that a good plan should try to accommodate both possibilities.

Obviously, this is a vastly oversimplified example. Real life is a little more complicated. But not always. Here's a real situation that closely mirrors this made-up example:

In 1999, my son Malcolm turned nine. For his birthday, he received a big hardcover novel from his aunt called *Harry Potter and the Chamber of Secrets*. Who was this Harry Potter fellow? Apparently, another book about Harry and his friends had already been published, but in 1999, neither Malcolm nor I had heard of him yet.

Two years later, the first Harry Potter movie came out, and as everybody now knows (unless you've been living under a rock), Harry Potter became a global phenomenon. Malcolm, like every kid his age, was enthralled. But for one reason or another, the book remained unread on his shelf.

Three more years passed, and more books and movies appeared in the series. One day, Malcolm excitedly announced that he'd been on the Internet and discovered that his Harry Potter book had become a collectors' item. It turned out that his birthday present happened to be a first edition—and books just like his were being sold online for the princely sum of $300!

"Fantastic!" I said. *"So, are you going to sell it?"*

for Witchcraft and Wizardry, second-year student Harry Potter finds himself in danger from a dark power that has once more been released on the school.
ISBN 0-439-06486-4
[1. Wizards — Fiction. 2. Magic — Fiction. 3. Schools — Fiction. 4. England — Fiction.] I. Title.
PZ7.R7968Har 1999
[Fic] — dc21 98-46370

10 9 8 7 6 5 4 3 2 1 9/9 0/0 1 2 3 4
Printed in the U.S.A. 37
First American edition, June 1999

Malcolm gave me one of those boy-Dad-are-you-ever-stupid looks. You see, he'd been doing some math. If the price of his book was $17.95 in 1999, and now (in 2004) it was worth $300, then it was a simple calculation to show that in 2014, the book's value would be $83,700. I may have raised an eyebrow at that point, but Malcolm carried on, unperturbed. "Dad, you won't believe it," he said, "but in 2024, the book will be worth $23,343,000! *I'll be rich*!" He began dancing around the room.

Alas, Malcolm had fallen into the dreaded extrapolation trap. (He had an excuse: He was 14.) The sad task fell to me to explain to him that yes, the value of the book had gone up very smartly since he first got it, but this linear growth wouldn't go on forever. Maybe, I suggested, he should work out a plan, a strategy, for getting the highest possible price for the book at some point in the future. I could help him. Why, we could conduct a scenario planning exercise!

So, that's what we did. First we defined our goal: to sell the book for as high a price as possible. In this sense, Malcolm's book was a kind of proxy for a "business" and we were trying to maximize its value. First, we had to define the value drivers of this business (i.e., the factors that determine its long-term chances of success). In Malcolm's case, that meant working out what conditions would have to be met for him to sell the book at the best price possible. Malcolm decided it all came down to two things: First, the book had to stay in pristine condition. That was the easy part; Malcolm was completely in control of the book's physical condition. The second factor was trickier, though. Harry Potter had to continue to be popular—wildly popular. How long would this remain the case? What popularity scenarios could unfold that would have an impact on the book's value?

We decided there were two likely scenarios for the future, a bit like the earlier example of red or yellow. Scenario one we called *Big Harry*. The Harry Potter phenomenon would stay big for the foreseeable future. In this scenario, the book would continue to go up in value.

Scenario two we called *Fade-Out*. Here, the Harry Potter phenomenon would diminish. In this case, the book would definitely go down in value—maybe very fast.

So, the flexible, value-maximizing strategy Malcolm had to pursue was now becoming clear. At the moment, with one blockbuster after another coming out, we were certainly experiencing the *Big Harry* scenario, so Malcolm's action plan was simply to keep the book safe and let its value go up and up on its own.

But sooner or later, *Fade-Out* would emerge—Harry Potter couldn't stay at the top of the best-seller lists forever. But when would this occur? We didn't know, but Malcolm had to be ready for it. And that meant reading the signals in the environment that would tell him when the scenarios were shifting.

We had to identify what those signals might be. Here's what we came up with. First, as long as J. K. Rowling kept publishing new Harry Potter books that became instant best sellers, Malcolm knew that *Big Harry* was still the operative scenario. So, one signal that would indicate the scenarios were shifting would be if a new Harry Potter book came out that didn't sell as well as the previous books.

Second, we figured that the movies played an even bigger role than the books in keeping the Harry Potter flame burning bright. If ticket sales for the Harry Potter movies were an even better proxy for his popularity than book sales, we should keep an eye on this. We decided that if the box office receipts from any Harry Potter movie on its first weekend after release were lower than for the previous movie in the series, this would mean that *Fade-Out* had started and that it was time to sell the book before its value started falling.

Last, we knew that eventually there *would* be a final Harry Potter movie. In 2004, when we were having this discussion, we didn't know when that would be. Could Ms. Rowling write five more books? Ten? Twenty? We had no idea, but we knew (sad as it was to admit) that it couldn't go on forever. On the assumption that the *Fade-Out* scenario would begin, at the latest, sometime after the last movie in the series was released, Malcolm decided he would sell his First Edition within two months after the final movie came out.

For the next seven years, the Harry Potter machine kept pumping out books and movies, right on schedule. Each film was a blockbuster, so Malcolm stuck to his strategy of merely holding onto the book. He checked the collectibles websites and, sure enough, the book's value kept rising.

Finally, in the summer of 2011, the last Harry Potter movie came out— *Harry Potter and the Deathly Hollows, Part 2*. In line with the plan we'd worked out way back in 2004, Malcolm, now a young man of 21, put the book up for sale on the Internet, and a few weeks later sold it for $1,600, or 89 times the 1999 retail price.

WHAT'S PLANNING ALL ABOUT, ANYWAY?

"I can't see the future, but I have to plan for it anyway." That's the CEO's classic dilemma.

How do you resolve this paradox? In a perfect world, the logical thing to do would be to predict the future. Just get that right, and everything else falls into place. Sounds so simple! But this isn't a perfect world. Down here on planet Earth, how can anyone even dream of predicting the future, when all around us, everything is in a state of constant and ever-accelerating change? Like it or not, the future is, and always will be, unknowable.

But just because it's fraught with uncertainty doesn't absolve you of your responsibility to plan for it. What's the first thing you should do, other than consoling yourself with a stiff whisky? In my opinion, your first task is to make a mental leap. It's to face, and accept, the hard fact that if absolute predictions are impossible (and they are), then planning based on absolute predictions is useless.

Once you've accepted this fact, then real planning can begin. By "real planning" I mean that you have let go of the attempt to figure out how the future *will* turn out and instead focus on understanding how the future *could* turn out. Depending on how countless trends develop, all of which are completely unknown today, things *could* turn out very differently. Or, to put it another way, several futures are possible. Having taken this critically important idea on board, you will then see that planning isn't a question of *predicting* the future but *preparing* for it—no matter which future actually unfolds.

In this new mental framework, the function of planning is to explore these possible futures and then confidently take the steps needed to improve your organization's flexibility and responsiveness to the different opportunities and threats these futures may bring your way. Exploration plus preparation: *That's* what planning's all about.

The New Highway

Have you ever heard a story like this?

Bill's gas station was a thriving business, the only service station on the old highway north of town. But then a new Interstate bypass was built on the south side of town, and nobody used the old road anymore. Within six months, Bill's went belly-up.

Sound familiar?

Is your business as vulnerable as Bill's gas station? It could be, if its success heavily depends on just one or two elements of the business environment that you have little control over. If those elements change in some unfavorable way—*poof!*—you're gone.

Think about your company's vulnerabilities. Do you suffer from a potential weak spot that could put you out of business if one or two external factors unexpectedly changed for the worse?

What's *your* "new highway"? Shouldn't you know what it is? And shouldn't you have a plan ready in case that scenario comes about?

"Our lives are defined by opportunities, even the ones we **miss.""**

F. Scott Fitzgerald

CHAPTER 2

HOW-TO

Rocket Science?

Not really.

How does scenario planning work in actual practice? Is it something that anyone can do, or do you need a doctorate in futurology, five years of apprenticeship at the feet of a master, nerves of steel, and a pilot's license?

The answer is that you can gain many of the basic benefits of scenario planning on your own, without adult supervision. However, as with any intellectual process, experience and expertise are very valuable when it comes to scenario planning, so even though it's not necessary to post a warning (e.g., "Do not try this at home!"), it's not a bad idea to have some expert help if you want to get the most out of it.

In this part of the book, we'll explore the process, and you'll see that it's possible to generate some solid scenario work without a PhD. (I will have to be careful not to give away too many trade secrets, though, or the International Brotherhood of Scenario Planners may send me a nasty letter. Or worse, revoke my membership.)

THE PROCESS

There is no fixed, here's-how-you-do-it rulebook for conducting a scenario planning process or workshop. There are a lot of variations, and many experts have developed their own proprietary approaches, so each exercise is likely to be somewhat different, depending on the preferred methodology and experience of the experts facilitating the discussion.

However, even though there's no one-size-fits-all approach, the scenario planning process as conducted by most experts usually proceeds according to a similar logic, which means....which means that it is likely to include some variation of the following six steps:

1. Framing the challenge
2. Gathering information
3. Identifying driving forces
4. Defining the future's critical "either/or" uncertainties
5. Generating the scenarios
6. Fleshing them out and creating story lines

By following this procedure, you will end up with a number of detailed scenarios. Now you have to do something with them, which requires an additional couple of steps if you want the scenarios to result in something of practical value:

7. Validating the scenarios and identifying further research needed
8. Assessing their implications and defining possible responses
9. Identifying signposts
10. Monitoring and updating the scenarios as time goes on

What this all comes down to is using the scenarios to help you develop a better strategic plan.

WHO IS INVOLVED?

Scenario planning is almost always done as a group exercise, with the group ranging anywhere from 9 or 10 up to perhaps 30 participants. One facilitator can handle a group of about a dozen; after that, it's advisable to have additional facilitators, as the process works best by breaking the group into smaller working teams for certain steps. Each team ought to have somebody hovering nearby to coach them.

Choosing the actual participants is an important task needing some real consideration. If the scenario planning is to have the greatest potential value, then the people who help create the scenarios should be open, intelligent, motivated, imaginative, and strategic thinkers.

But that's not all! They also need to be good communicators—able to formulate ideas and also to explain them clearly to the others. The group also needs to include people who represent different perspectives and interests. This diversity of experience and point of view is crucial. Without it, there can be a tendency for the group to fall in line with the thinking of the boss. Having other stakeholders involved keeps everybody true to their interests and viewpoints.

Last, the people chosen to participate in a scenario planning exercise should be individuals who are well respected. This point cannot be overemphasized. Within the group, you cannot afford to have participants whom the others don't find credible, or whose contribution to the various discussions will already be discounted before they even open their mouths. This doesn't mean that everyone has to be a senior vice president. (In fact, it's better if everyone is *not* a senior vice president.) But even if nine hierarchical levels separate the highest-ranking member of the group from the lowest-ranking member, *all* of the participants need to have respect for each other's position and opinions.

Another important reason for assuring that the group consists of individuals who command some respect is to make buy-in easier when the results are communicated to the rest of the organization, the public, or other stakeholders. Remember that scenario planning is a tool that ultimately helps you make big decisions about the future direction of your organization. That means a lot is potentially at stake, for many people. When they are

first exposed to the scenario planning results, it's natural that some people may conclude that they will be big "winners" in the future; others will see themselves as "losers." A well-respected scenario planning team can dispel this idea. . . or, as the case may be, make bad news easier to swallow.

STEP 1. FRAMING THE CHALLENGE

There are many reasons why an organization would turn to scenario planning to help it assess how the future could develop and to better understand what its options are. All of these reasons are likely to be related in some way to its strategy, but it's possible to apply scenario planning at a number of different levels in order to gain insight to different kinds of challenges.

The most general and wide-ranging application for scenario planning is simply to reveal insights into future opportunities (and threats) that would affect the organization's overarching **mission**:

- *Industry association.* What are the possibilities for the future of our industry?
- *An emerging market nation.* As a country, how should we be investing to boost export growth over the next 20 years?
- *A wine grower.* What is the outlook for our company's product portfolio, given the changes taking place in our markets?
- *The governor and his or her planning team.* How will continued urban development in our state affect our traditional agricultural base over the next decade?

An organization may want to explore the scenarios that would be relevant only to a specific **project** or **goal**:

- *A health food company.* How can we introduce our best-selling product in a new geographic market?
- *A hotel chain.* What would be the best way for us to become more competitive in our recruitment and hiring?

- *A sporting goods manufacturer.* What are our options for maintaining our number one position in the United Kingdom?
- *The city council of Nowheresville, USA.* How can we get buy-in from the townsfolk to build a bigger airport?

Another reason scenario planning could make sense would be to search for solutions to a particular **crisis situation**:

- *An airline.* A low-cost competitor just launched a service on our most profitable route. How should we respond?
- *A regional bank.* How will the new banking laws just enacted affect our ability to compete with larger institutions?
- *A specialty manufacturer.* The cost of our most important raw material is going through the roof. What could this mean for our future strategy?

Any number of situations can readily justify the use of scenario planning to explore alternative outcomes so that an organization can define the most flexible strategies and pragmatic solutions. The key is to frame the exercise to try to answer questions such as those in the preceding lists. The outcome of a scenario planning exercise called "What could we do about this problem we're facing?" will yield much more practical insights than one called "The future: Aren't you just dying to know what it will be like?"

Another important aspect of framing the problem to be explored is to define the *time horizon*. Be sure to choose a time scale in which the strategic solutions and plans you develop can fully be implemented—and show results!

It might also be useful to define the *stakeholders* involved, both in the challenge and in the solution. They may or may not be participants in the process, but you will be able to frame the challenge more comprehensively if you clearly understand their stake in it.

Last, even at this early stage of the process (*especially* at this early stage), a little *shock value* can pay dividends in focus, motivation, and later, creativity. Don't hesitate to frame the challenge in a negative way, as in the following examples.

Living with our undersized airport:
Where will this leave Nowheresville in 2025?

The 2020 banking landscape under the new regulatory framework:
What if the big boys come to town?

Get the attention of the participants and stakeholders!

STEP 2. INFORMATION GATHERING

You cannot create a coherent future scenario without understanding (or at least knowing something about) the key trends that are happening now and that, in the fullness of time, will affect your organization and will give the scenarios their contours, if not their shape and color.

So, you are going to have to do some homework.

Ideally, you'll have as much data about the challenge you're trying to address as possible. However, as you can see from the preceding examples, one problem to be explored may be very different from another, so there is no single checklist that will help you gather all the information you may need.

In one of the preceding examples, you'll want to know as much about your competitors as you can—their strengths and weaknesses, their product portfolios, market shares, and geographic reach, strategies and capabilities, maybe even a profile of key members of their management teams, including their backgrounds and expertise.

In another example, it's not the competition that is causing alarm, but the cost of raw materials, so you would want to have data on commodity

and transport prices, the outlook for availability, and an understanding of the forces driving those particular prices higher, which may range from political and regulatory issues, production bottlenecks, and possibly supply disruptions to evolving sources of increased (or decreased) demand. Perhaps profiles of the largest companies extracting those commodities would also be relevant.

This kind of information provides a useful basis for only one side of the story of the future, though. Information is also needed about what could happen in the future, that is, the trends and developments that *could* have an impact of some kind on the challenge you've defined and your ability to meet it.

Which trends are relevant? The answer is, "That depends." Almost anything *could* be relevant, especially since the objective of the entire exercise is to think outside the box. In that case, it can be instructive to explore less obvious cause-and-effect relationships. Your future will be affected by many forces whose impact is only *indirect*. In this phase of the process, you'll want to imagine what those could be.

Information gathering can be a long, even tedious, process. But it's important. Anticipating the need for solid information about how their organization's value drivers are developing, many scenario planners collect detailed trend information on a permanent basis, establishing libraries and databases (or at least large manila folders) devoted to the developments they consider the most important for their future. Ongoing data gathering and evaluation obviates the need to run around in a mad rush trying to find useful information shortly before a scenario planning exercise gets under way, but it obviously requires time and resources.

But what if you don't have these? Not every organization has the wherewithal to support a staff whose permanent mission is to dig for data on a dozen or more trends and developments. How can you zero in quickly on the most essential factors that could prove influential—even critical—to your future success?

The best way is through personal interviews. These are so useful that I recommend scenario planners conduct interviews even if they also have an extensive library available of excellent, unimpeachable data. Interviewees bring subjective opinion and subtle judgment into the equation, but also imagination and blue-sky thinking—all based on experience. All of these things are valuable.

Who to interview? What to ask? Identify a number of knowledgeable, opinionated people—preferably stakeholders in your future success, or people with an interest in how your environment will develop. How many interviews should you conduct? Cast your net as widely as you can. You should talk to at least as many people as there will be in the group that will meet to carry out the scenario planning exercise; some planners recommend a ratio of three or even five interviewees to one workshop participant.

When interviewing these knowledgeable experts, your objective is to get a feeling for how they see the future developing in a general sense, as well as for your specific business, project, or product. Ask them such questions as:

- Looking at the future as an optimist, in what ways do you think the world will be different 10 years from now compared to today?
- How about if you looked at the world as a pessimist?
- How do you think our future business/market environment will change during that time?
- What changes need to happen if our industry/company/project is to be successful 10 years from now?
- How do you think the products offered by us and our competitors will be different in 10 years compared to today?
- How might our customers be different? What might they expect from our company and our products that we don't deliver today?
- Who do you think our most important competitors will be 10 years from now?

Perhaps the single most important question you can ask your interviewees is this one:

> If you could see 10 years into the future, what two or three things would you look for that would help you understand how the future has turned out?

This is a quick-and-dirty way to find out what your interviewees think are the critically important changes ahead—watershed developments that your organization will have to confront and master in order to be successful in the future. You will get some insightful, maybe even eye-opening, replies to the preceding question. For example,

> "I'd look at people's cell phones—how they're used compared to today, what kinds of apps are on them, how they've evolved, how people use them most."

> "I'd like to know about the age structure of the population, especially if people are living a lot longer than before, and something about the quality of life of these old people."

> "I'd want to see whether there are still a lot of political disagreements about taxes and entitlements. Is the retirement age still the same? I'd want to know if the outlook for the Social Security system has been resolved. (Something tells me it will still be a mess.)"

> "I'd want to find out whether university enrollment's gone up or whether online education has become more important."

Volcanic Plumes and Scuba Vacations

What Kind of Information Is Relevant?

In mid-April 2010, a volcano on the south coast of Iceland with the daunting name of Eyjafjallajökull erupted, sending a plume of ash 30,000 feet up into the air—and right into the jet stream, which carried it directly toward continental Europe.

The volcanic ash contained very fine particles of silica, which posed a real risk to jet engines of airplanes. Pilots could find that, having sucked ash into the intake, their plane's engines would shut down—not something you want to experience when cruising six miles above the Earth.

As the ash cloud spread, one European country after another closed its airspace to jet travel, citing the safety risk to air travelers. Seven days after the eruption, 107,000 flights had been canceled to, from, and within Europe, leaving 5 million passengers stranded worldwide. Many were unable to leave the airports where their flights were grounded, as they had no visas for the countries in which they were stuck. It was the largest shutdown of air traffic since World War II.

One business that is heavily dependent on airlift from Europe is Indian Ocean tourism. For vacationers from Berlin, Brussels, or Barcelona, such gorgeous island destinations as Mauritius, the Maldives, and the Seychelles are unreachable without air connections, and for that week in 2010, there were none. No one could get there from Europe.

Most hotels can (and did) survive a week of cancellations, but what if the next time a volcano blows, it keeps belching ash into the air for three months? Could a volcanic eruption in Iceland cause a hotel to go bust in the Seychelles?

It doesn't seem beyond the realm of possibility, does it? Does that mean that scenario planners for a hotel company in the Seychelles should collect geological reports on expected future volcanic activity in Iceland? What about volcanoes in the rest of the world? Do the planners also need meteorological data so they can understand how the ash cloud (from any volcano on earth, mind you) is likely to spread? And don't forget information on developments in jet engine design: Someone, somewhere, is bound to be working on an engine that can withstand volcanic ash, and won't it be great when that's a reality?

Is all this relevant? In spite of a r eal-life case where a volcano actually did cause business losses on the other side of the world, the answer is no. Volcanic activity (at least for now, thank goodness) is not a trend, and therefore not a true value driver affecting the hotel business in the Indian Ocean, or anywhere else, with the probable exception of hotels built on the actual slope of a volcano, but I'm not familiar with any such hotels (and wouldn't stay in one if I were). Rather than a trend, this is an instance of what is called a black swan event: low probability, high impact. We look at black swan events in more detail later.

STEP 3. IDENTIFYING DRIVING FORCES

Now we come to the workshop itself, the crucible in which the participants meet, discuss, argue, and (we hope) finally agree on certain key attributes of the future and craft scenarios based on these choices.

The previous two tasks, framing the challenge and gathering relevant information, are completed beforehand. (Information gathering may never actually be "completed," as in some companies it will be an ongoing process.) The present step, identifying present and future driving forces, is likely to be the first item of real business on the agenda when the entire group gets together.

What exactly is a *driving force*? In a nutshell, a driving force is something with the potential to bring about significant change in the future. It may be a trend, already clearly defined and understood—for example, the falling fertility rate in Italy, which will have a fairly predictable impact on the number of Italians who will be 20 years old two decades from now.

Another kind of driving force is a variable that has the potential to change the future in significant ways but is not very predictable as it is itself dependent on several factors. A good example is the price of oil. Everyone would agree that the price of a barrel of oil affects the cost of many other products and services, from food to airline tickets; it affects the demand for cars at both ends of the gas-guzzling spectrum; and it has an impact on overall economic growth.

But the price of oil is driven by a combination of supply and demand factors. In 1973, for example, OPEC tightly controlled the world's petroleum spigot and engineered a quadrupling of oil prices, from $3 to $12 a barrel (those were the good old days).

That was supply-driven change. Forty years later, however, the oil market is primarily demand-driven. In the six years before 2008, for example, the price of oil rose from about $15 a barrel to over $140 a barrel, thanks largely to increased demand from China's roaring economy. But in 2008, unexpect-

edly, a worldwide recession began and economic activity levels fell—along with demand for oil. The price collapsed, from $140 to $35, in six months.

Here we see the price of oil as a definite driving force—a major source of change—but one that is highly uncertain.

The classic tool for helping generate a list of driving forces is the "PEST" model. A scenario planning group will be asked to think of relevant forces at work in their industry, company, project, whatever from among these four categories:

Political
Economic
Societal
Technological

There are other models out there that include additional categories, such as "Environmental" (which turns PEST into STEEP). Probably the most exhaustive one that I've seen breaks driving forces down into a whopping 10 categories:

Social
Technological
Economic
Business methods
Natural resources
Political
Demographic
International
Legal
Environmental

However, "STEBNPDILE" is a bit difficult to remember, so even though it's a more thorough checklist, this model might be more unwieldy to use in practice.

No matter which acronym you choose to help participants brainstorm, the point is to call upon the brainpower in the room to develop a list of as many driving forces as possible that are potentially significant for the company's fortunes between now and the agreed time horizon—usually 10 years, sometimes longer.

A typical workshop might easily generate 100 or more driving forces. Many will be interrelated, with one of them causing, or affecting, another. For example, let's imagine a casino in Las Vegas determining its driving forces. Seeing the increasing importance of its British clientele, the scenario planning participants would include the following as one of its driving forces:

$\rightarrow$ *Popularity of Las Vegas in the United Kingdom*

All well and good. But popularity alone is not the whole story. Closely related would be this:

$\rightarrow$ *Las Vegas's reputation in the UK market*

This in turn is driven in part by the following factors:

$\rightarrow$ *Vegas's marketing and PR efforts in the UK*

$\rightarrow$ *Size of marketing and PR budget*

But there's more to consider:

$\rightarrow$ *Ease and affordability of air links from British airports*

This depends on:

$\rightarrow$ *Frequency of direct flights from London or Manchester to Vegas*

$\rightarrow$ *Price of round-trip airfare*

And this of course partly depends on:

$\rightarrow$ *Cost of jet fuel*

This brings us back to:

$\rightarrow$ *Price of a barrel of oil*

This is therefore a driving force for the casino as well.

Once all the driving forces have been derived (usually scribbled on Post-it notes so they can be shuffled around), group them into interdependent clusters, as in the casino example. The "UK visitors" cluster could include all of the driving forces shown earlier, as well as:

$\rightarrow$ *Strength of the British economy*

$\rightarrow$ *Exchange rate of the British pound*

You could even make a case that these last factors depend on:

$\rightarrow$ *UK monetary policy*

$\rightarrow$ *Which party has a majority in Parliament*

What's important is to try to see patterns of interaction—linkages of cause and effect—that may take place in combination or one after the other, to create a certain set of conditions in the future that will affect you.

The more, the better

EITHER ←

OR

STEP 4. DEFINING THE FUTURE'S CRITICAL "EITHER/OR" UNCERTAINTIES

Now it's time to home in on the key unknowns for the future—the ones that can make the biggest difference. The clusters of driving forces derived in the previous step help you identify what these might be.

The world is full of uncertainties. Is there any company or organization on earth that could realistically look at the next 10 years and expect no change? None that I can think of. Most CEOs, if asked to pick two words to describe their companies' business environment, would not put "stability" and "predictability" on their list!

That's not to say that all uncertainties are created equal. There are many things we don't know with 100 percent certainty about the future, but we do know enough to make an educated guess. Demographic changes, for example, are largely predetermined by long-term trends. Their *degree of*

uncertainty is very low. Not so with many other trends (e.g., new technologies), which may come screaming out of the blue, taking the market and the world by complete surprise.

In addition, for any given organization, some of the uncertainties about the future are more important than others. Their *potential impact* is greater. If I'm planning a picnic two weeks from Saturday, two uncertainties I will be confronted with are the weather and the pesky, ever-fluctuating price of cheese. Neither is known, but the weather will have a far greater impact on the success of my outing than how much I have to pay for the cheese.

Given these facts of life about the uncertainties you're facing—their varying degree and varying importance—the scenario planning exercise will yield the most valuable results if it ignores the less interesting driving forces and their outcomes and focuses on the critical extremes (i.e., the highly uncertain, potentially high-impact developments).

Why is this the case? Remember, one of the purposes of scenario planning is to think about the unthinkable. Where is the value to you if the scenario planning restricts its scope to examining the changes that are relatively sure to take place—and of relatively little importance to you if they do?

To identify the critical uncertainties, it helps to plot them on a graph like the one on the right.

Brings the contrast between alternative futures into sharper focus

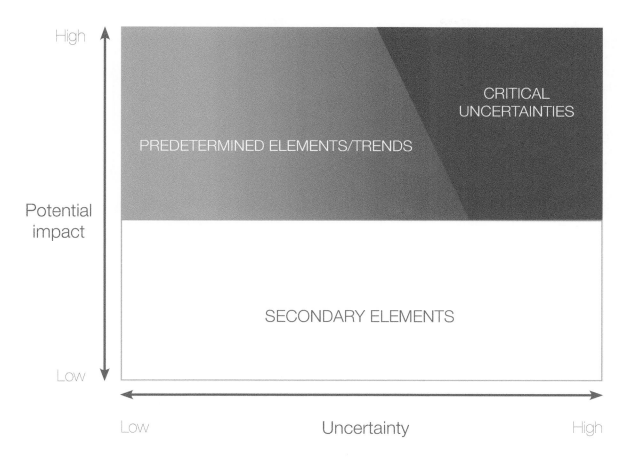

Each of the driving forces, or clusters of driving forces, from the previous step should now be plotted on this graph in order to visualize its relevance, or "interestingness." The goal is to identify the two most critical uncertainties, i.e., the two driving forces, trends, or developments that combine the greatest degree of uncertainty with the greatest potential impact on the future success of the organization or the outcome of the project.

The group may well argue about where each driving force belongs on the graph, and that's as it should be. The process should generate discussion, even disagreement. Eventually, however, it's necessary to decide on the two factors that are the most critical given the time horizon that's been agreed on. This last point is important to remember, because almost any trend or driving force could be relatively unimportant if you are looking only at a five-year time horizon, yet of absolutely crucial significance 20 years from now. The same goes for its relative uncertainty.

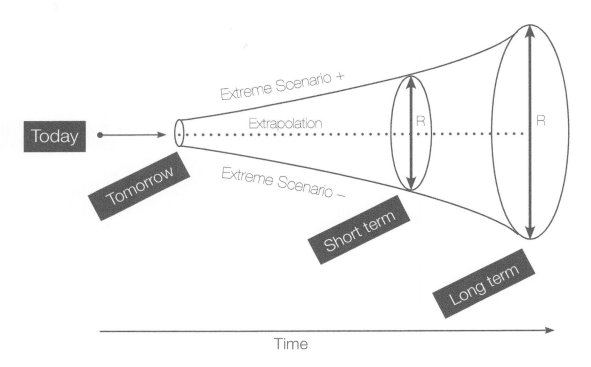

R = Range of possible outcomes

As time goes on, the range of possible future outcomes becomes greater (i.e. there is greater uncertainty what will happen). At the same time, trends have had time to pick up momentum, so they may have greater potential to have an impact.

In the example that follows, the group would eliminate driving forces/ clusters A, B, and C, as these unambiguously represent uncertainties that are less interesting as far as your future is concerned. They are the equivalent of the not-so-important price of cheese for the picnic planned (A or B) and demographic trends that may have a big impact on your organization in the long term but are relatively certain to take place (C).

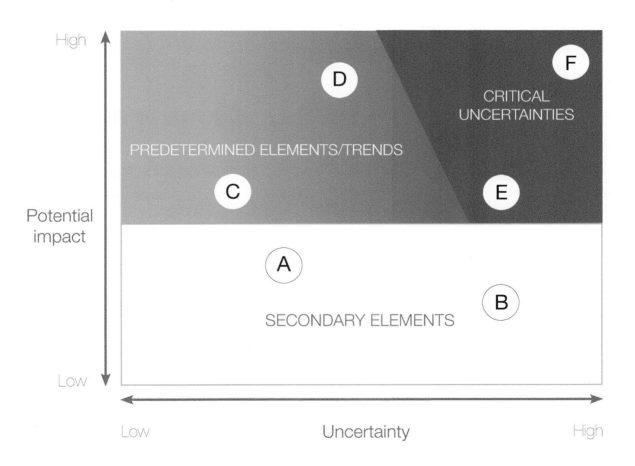

There may be some discussion about whether D, which among the six driving forces has been ranked second in terms of its possible impact, ought to be considered as one of the two critical uncertainties. Instead, driving forces E and F are selected, as both are considered high-uncertainty, high-impact, even though E is possibly less important than D.

Having selected E and F as the critical uncertainties, the next step is to create a new graph, a classic 2 × 2 matrix with E and F as the axes. The four quadrants of this graph now define the basic contours of four different future scenarios. Each one is defined in terms of an "either/or" outcome for the two critical uncertainties.

In other words, the four quadrants—we can already call them scenarios—are defined by whether driving force E will be either "high" or "low," for example, and whether, at the same time, driving force F will be either "big" or "small."

In real life, not every trend results in nice, clean, either/or, black-or-white outcome. Shades of gray predominate. But in order to construct scenarios that have the narrative power to illuminate stark differences between alternative futures, it's important to think of the two critical uncertainties as delineating two either/or situations at the same time.

For example, the cost of energy could be a critical uncertainty for companies in many different industries. The axis delineating this key dimension would not try to pinpoint particular price levels but instead would simply separate the future into two possible outcomes:

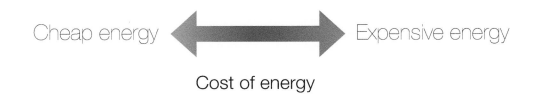

Cheap energy — Expensive energy

Cost of energy

Likewise, we might see dimensions such as these considered the critical uncertainties for organizations ranging from manufacturers to banks to schools:

Relaxed — Strict

Regulatory environment

Domestic market — International markets

Primary growth market

Traditional methods dominate — Technology-based methods dominate

Educational tools and techniques

STEP 5. GENERATING THE SCENARIOS

Actually creating scenarios is simple at this point. The two axes are combined, for example, like this:

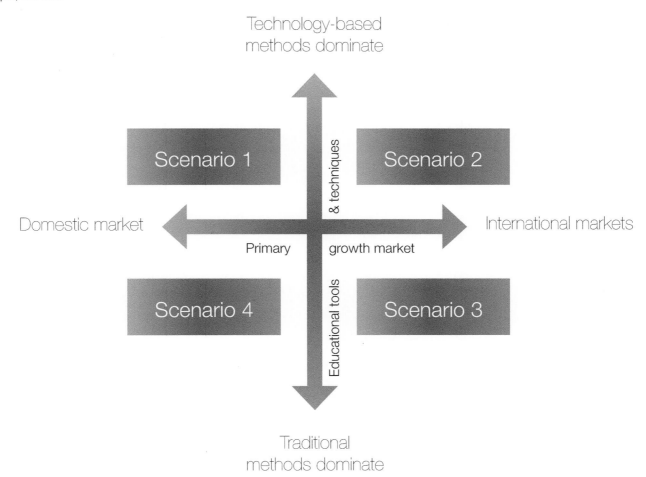

Technology-based
methods dominate

& techniques

Scenario 1

Scenario 2

Domestic market

International markets

Primary   growth market

Educational tools

Scenario 4

Scenario 3

Traditional
methods dominate

The result is a **scenario cross**, a matrix in which the four quadrants represent four different scenarios. The preceding one might be valid, for example, for a university trying to peer into its future. According to the matrix, the four critically different scenarios would be:

1. The majority of students come from the school's home country (and presumably its familiar feeder schools), while new educational tools based on technological developments change the classroom experience (and probably also the teacher-student working relationship, research techniques, homework assignments, etc.).

2. More students come from abroad (with implications for the institution's fee revenues, culture and values, possible changes in curriculum and faculty, changing needs of students and their families, etc.), while the educational experience also changes with new technological advances and tools.

3. The number of international students is growing, while the school's way of doing business remains primarily the tried-and-true methods the educational field has always used (and still uses). Technological advances continue, but they haven't substantially changed the dynamic of the classroom, which still relies on professorial talent and the traditional relationship between teacher and student.

4. New students are mostly domestic, and the school's teaching methods, faculty, and capabilities continue to be based on familiar structures and tools.

As you might imagine, an institution of higher education facing these four possible futures could see potentially enormous differences between them in many aspects of its mission and day-to-day existence, such as:

- How it would position and market itself
- The role it might (should?) play in student life
- The ideal profile of future faculty members
- The changing sources of possible donations
- Investments to be made in technology
- Evolving relations with alumni
- Changing expectations of employers
- The vulnerability of its tuition stream

It isn't necessary, but it's a good idea to give the scenarios a name. A good name can really capture the essence of that particular future; besides, coming up with a catchy name is fun, motivates the group, and makes the exercise a little more human and less daunting. (And the scenarios are easier to remember.)

Titles of songs, books, or movies work well

So perhaps the university's scenarios would be labeled as shown in this graphic:

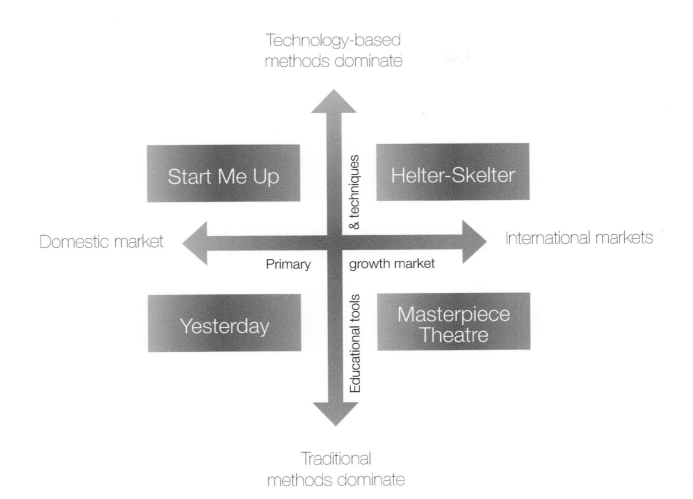

"Wouldn't *That* Be a Great Scenario!"

When the Tail Wags the Dog

Not long ago, I was meeting with the management team responsible for running the European branch campus of an American university. They prided themselves on the depth of their three-year strategic plans, and now I was trying to convince them that a scenario planning exercise would help them see a bit further out than that. It could help them in several ways, I said. For example, the process could give them some insights into how the business world might change over the next few years, which could affect the demand for different kinds of degree programs and structures they could offer. This understanding could allow them to improve the quality of their long-range curriculum development plans.

I thought they were beginning to see the light, when one of the school's directors chimed in with a question. "We've never done much fund-raising," he said, "but for the first time, we're pretty close to landing a major dona-tion. It would be about $10 million—a huge amount of money for us. There's so much we could do with a gift that size: hire new faculty, upgrade the dorms, build new facilities. . . . So, if we do this workshop with you, could we be sure to include a scenario in which we get this money?" Around the table, everyone nodded in consensus, "Yes, that's absolutely a scenario we need to consider. We definitely want that to happen."

I asked when the donor was going to make a decision. "We'll know within the next five or six months," the director replied. The subject of this big gift to the school had brought a palpable sense of excitement into the discus-sion; everyone seemed keyed up about it. I duly noted it and wrote it down, but inside, I knew what this question really meant: I hadn't managed to get the group to grasp what the scenario planning process should, and should not, try to address. I was sure that this "What if we Win the Lottery?" scenario wouldn't really help them gain any insights into their long-term future.

But why wouldn't it? After all, the school's directors were not wrong to think about their chances of getting that donation or how to spend it if and when they did. To them, it made perfect sense as a future scenario—at that moment, it was clearly the one thing that had the biggest potential impact on the school's future. In fact, as the conversation went on, their whole world seemed to boil down to just two future scenarios: (1) We get that cash, or (2) We don't. It seemed obvious that at that stage of our discussions, the directors saw scenario planning as a process that would show them how that hoped-for-but-as-yet-uncollected money would change things in the future.

This is an example of why scenario planning needs to take a longer-term view, and a broader view of the entire competitive environment, if it is go-ing to be useful for an organization. My immediate task was to switch gears and get these university directors to see that, whether they got that money or not, the world in which they would be operating would be changing over the next few years and that scenario planning could help them see the different landscapes that could be developing. Then, *and only then*, should they apply these insights to the process of deciding what to do with an extra 10 million bucks that might fall into their laps. At the same time, I explained, the scenario process should also help them make plans in case the donation didn't materialize.

In other words, the key to success for the school is not so much the size of its bank account, but how well it adapts to the changing environment in which it operates, no matter how much money it has. The bank account may be flush with moola or in a state of permanent overdraft (or fluctuate between the two), but either way, the environment will be what it is, and the school will have to do business in that environment with whatever funds it has. Of course, it's always better to have $10 million in the bank than nothing, but having $10 million doesn't change what's going on in your business landscape—it only changes what you're able to do about it.

The best thing the scenario planning process could do for them would be to get as far away as possible from the two possibilities that were momentarily coloring their perception of the future—"Rich as Croesus" versus "Business as Usual"—and focus on the world they would have to compete in 10 years down the line, irrespective of the donation.

The process would therefore focus on identifying the value drivers for the university and imagining how they might change. Scenarios would be generated based on clustering these in a sensible way and then seeing the either/or outcomes the future could hold if these clusters, or major dimensions, tended toward one direction or the other.

The result, I explained, should be that the university would be in a better position to assess how a $10 million gift might best be invested. Not only that, it might also reveal the outlines of a future in which more donations like that could be attainable, thanks to understanding economic conditions, attitudes toward giving, and so on. Based on the scenarios, the school could begin to formulate a set of arguments that they could put in front of potential donors to gain their buy-in and help them understand how the school's vision and long-term plans would be in line with the way the world is changing.

This reasoning eventually won the day. But the story is a good example of a typical misunderstanding—namely, that for some people, future scenarios should be force-fit to match specific events (or even a wished-for condition) that they think could or should, come about. Doing this is no longer *exploring* the future; it's *prejudicing* it. It's letting the tail wag the dog and should be avoided whenever possible.

STEP 6. FLESHING THEM OUT AND CREATING STORY LINES

The scenarios now have parameters and names.

What comes next is to expand the basic idea of each one and add meat to the bones. This is the part of the process that calls upon creativity and imagination the most.

Taking a basic scenario description, for example "Helter-Skelter," the group fleshes it out by asking questions such as:

- What does it mean for the university that other countries have become the primary source of new students?
- Who and what will be affected, and how?
- What does it mean financially?
- What might it mean for the daily life of the school?
- How will the school have to adapt?

At the same time—looking at the second aspect of that scenario:

- What are the implications for a change in the way teaching and learning take place, leaning more on technological tools than on traditional methods?
- What are the advantages and disadvantages of this change?
- What will the school have to watch out for?
- How much will it cost?
- What could be the impact on the quality of the education delivered?
- What will be the impact on the reputation of the school and the degrees conferred?

The ideal result is a description of the future end state, a detailed picture of what that world looks like and feels like—along with a story explaining how it came into being (i.e., the developments taking place over the next 10 years that lead to that end state).

It should explain what that end state is like from the perspective of different stakeholders, too. This helps in understanding what their priorities may be and what issues could arise because of their likely perception of the way the future has turned out. There may be winners and losers in a particular scenario, and it's important to understand who will be in each category, and why, and how they might react to being there (not to mention how they might react today to learning that they might be winners or losers in the future).

In actual fact, the story is told backward. If the time horizon is 10 years, then the narrative begins in the year 2025, for example, and creates a plausible explanation accounting for the changes over the decade leading up to 2025. Looking back from that future vantage point, what happened during the previous 10 years that resulted in the future looking like the one described by "Helter-Skelter"? How, exactly, did that world come about?

Very often, scenario planning groups are able to come up with a fictional chronology of events or milestones (e.g., "In 2019, we noticed for the first time that there were more foreign students than Americans in the freshman intake"), but what is more important is to describe the *chain of causality*. What should emerge from this important phase of the scenario planning process should be more than a canned timeline of the next 10 years; it should be a more in-depth "history" of the next 10 years—a logical, step-by-step reasoning of the intermediate causes and effects that resulted, in 10 years, in that particular end state coming into being.

This needs to be done for all four scenarios—obviously a job that needs more time than a rushed 45 minutes at the end of a two-day workshop, when everyone is exhilarated but exhausted. It's best to reconvene the group to attack this task fresh, maybe even allowing everyone a few weeks to cogitate on the possibilities and discuss them over the watercooler. Scenario planning is a deliberative process, and the results will be better if the process is spread out over time, with enough of a gap between steps to allow the ideas to marinade a little.

In any event, the history writing process can be a bumpy one. Giving a team of people the job of concocting four pieces of creative writing is an interesting experience, and even enthusiastic participants can become frustrated when their work isn't flowing smoothly from their pens. Needless to say, fiction drafted by a committee is rarely as gripping as *The Da Vinci Code*.

These concerns don't really matter. A good facilitator can prompt a writing team to roll up their sleeves and craft a realistic chain of events that would bring a particular scenario into being. But some legitimate difficulties can crop up, which may be symptoms of a weakness in the foregoing analysis that should then be revisited.

For example, if the teams are having trouble developing any kind of story at all, or one that doesn't seem to respect the boundaries between the scenarios, mixing elements from different scenarios instead of crisply sticking to the parameters as defined, it could be because the two critical uncertainties that were chosen are too vague, or perhaps the binary aspect is not clear enough; the *either* is too much like the *or*. The problem could also be that there is too close a relationship between the two critical uncertainties. They need to be independent of each other; if they tend to move together, both up or both down, or if uncertainty 1 causes uncertainty 2, then go back to the drawing board and define a new pair.

It's also a good idea to change the composition of the teams working on the four write-ups, rotating the members through all four. This helps avoid the possibility that a team comes to be associated with one scenario ("So you're the Helter-Skelter guys") or becomes attached to its scenario and wants it to be "the best." The outcome should be that the entire group of participants proudly takes ownership of all four scenarios, not just the one that they happened to have written up. It isn't a competition!

STEP 7. VALIDATING THE SCENARIOS AND IDENTIFYING FURTHER RESEARCH NEEDED

After all the creative juices have flowed and the scenarios have been drafted, but before they have been made official or have been widely distributed, they should be thoroughly vetted by knowledgeable outsiders to the process. Ideally, you will present the scenarios to a selection of stakeholders and other individuals with relevant experience or expertise and ask for their feedback:

- Are the scenarios plausible?
- Are they clear?
- Are they relevant?
- Do they seem internally consistent?
- What's missing?
- What changes should be made?

Collect the comments from these experts and integrate them into the scenarios wherever possible. They may also spot some weaknesses in the scenarios—for example, insufficiently thought-out conceptual elements that could stand some additional research to shore them up. This is invaluable feedback. Do the homework and make the adjustments.

Very important !

STEP 8. ASSESSING THEIR IMPLICATIONS AND DEFINING POSSIBLE RESPONSES

There are several ways to do this. The critical thing to accomplish, though, is to develop a catalog of possible strategic options for each of the scenarios. If the future really turns out to look like this, how would the group want the company to react?

Generating options is followed by evaluating them. Here, it's possible to cluster the various responses into a smaller number of broader strategic options. Then, undoubtedly following a great deal of discussion, a choice needs to be made: Which strategy makes the most sense?

From a scenario planning point of view, the best strategy is the one that gives the organization the greatest degree of flexibility. As the future takes shape (whichever future it happens to be), you will want room to maneuver.

STEP 9. IDENTIFYING SIGNPOSTS

The scenarios you've created each define a world that could exist 10 years from now, or even more. The four scenarios (i.e., the four "worlds" you've described) are each different, yet they've all been vetted, and everyone involved in the process is in agreement that from today's vantage point, they are all plausible. That doesn't mean that everyone believes each scenario has a 25 percent probability of emerging. But possible? You betcha.

This implies that from today's starting point, developments could take you in any one of the four directions defined. For the moment, you simply don't know which of those directions it will be.

So, an important question is, when *will* you know? A year from now, many things will already be different. Based on the changes over the previous 12 months, will it be possible to see more clearly that one of the

scenarios is emerging rather than the other three? If not, how about in three years? Or five? Surely there comes a point where the fog lifts and it becomes clear where we're heading.

Of course, the answer to this question is that the future doesn't reveal itself according to a timetable. Instead, it can only be read (to the extent it can be read at all) by noticing the events and changes that take place along the way. That is what you have to be able to do: Read the signs.

Before you can do this, the scenario planning team should look at the scenarios and try to figure out, for each one, what those signs are likely to be. They won't be as obvious as this:

However, you should be able to identify plenty of indicators that potentially signal a particular scenario emerging, from major geopolitical events and election results to economic data and new legislation. And that is just the front-page stuff. More subtle indicators could include anything from shifts in consumer moods, behavior, or fashion to the appearance of new kinds of products or services that potentially herald an eventual industry upheaval.

"What could tell us that this scenario is emerging?" is a question that should be asked of all four, and as many answers as possible should be logged and kept at the forefront for future reference.

As you'll see in the case study on VisitScotland, the scenario planning group exploring the future of Scottish tourism realized that one of their scenarios was emerging when they saw on the evening news that heavily armed British soldiers would begin patrolling Heathrow Airport. Subtle or not so subtle, hundreds of such signposts are out there to be read if you keep your eyes open.

STEP 10. MONITORING AND UPDATING THE SCENARIOS

Time does not stand still. The final phase in the scenario planning process is a permanent one: to keep the scenarios updated. That primarily means keeping abreast of changes in your business environment that correspond to elements in the scenarios, particularly the driving forces. Not a difficult process, but one that requires time and resources.

On a regular basis—once a year should do it—the scenario planning group, or perhaps a smaller working group, should get together to evaluate the changes, note the signposts that have been passed along the way, and recommend changes to the scenarios and strategy, as required.

> **"You know what's weird? Day by day, nothing seems to change. But pretty soon, everything's different."**
>
> *Calvin and Hobbes* (Bill Watterson)

Once upon a future...

The new product was an instant success...

It was a letter from a law firm in New York...

Their biggest rival went under in 2019...

Vignettes: Bringing the Future to Life

The histories have been written and edited (then argued over, rewritten, and reedited, etc.). The results are eye-opening, as good scenarios should be. Everyone is pleased.

The creative work is not yet finished, though. Now comes some real fun.

To dramatize the look and feel of a future scenario, the group should give its most imaginative writers a special assignment: to concoct a brief "day-in-the-life" vignette for each scenario.

Based on elements of fiction—characters, setting, a simple plot—these four scenes can vividly demonstrate the scenarios' impact on the organization by revealing how a fictitious person in the future thinks and behaves, how he or she perceives and interacts with other important parts of the future environment—in short, what effects the future world is having on that person.

The person might be an employee, a customer, a supplier, or some other stakeholder. The key is that, through this person's eyes, we gain a nuanced vision of the future, warts and all.

The individual does not have to be the same person in all four vignettes. The four stories should be crafted so that the characters and plots manage to bring out the essential flavor of that future for the organization. To do this, perhaps one story is best told through the eyes of a supplier to your company; in another, maybe the future is brought into sharper focus by telling a story about how one of the company's salespeople spends a typical day.

Following are two examples of scenario vignettes written for "Bank Bärtobel," a fictitious Swiss private bank that wanted to explore the world of 2025. The bank's scenario planning group came up with two critical uncertainties:

1. Would economic development over the next decade lead to a world of global prosperity, or would a sclerotic Europe and America remain relatively stagnant while wealth creation was more concentrated in areas such as the BRICs?

2. Would Switzerland's by then 90-year-old laws protecting financial privacy still be in place in 2025? The answer to this question would depend on how much the Swiss government and public felt that the banking industry deserved support.

Bank Bärtobel's business environment in the year 2025

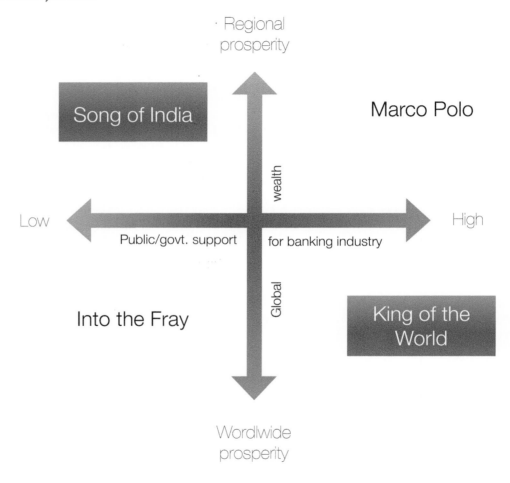

Based on the two driving forces mentioned previously, the bank developed the four scenarios to the left. Following are the vignettes written for two of these scenarios, "Song of India" and "King of the World." As you can see, the two worlds envisioned could not be more different.

SCENARIO: "SONG OF INDIA"

Hans Zimmermann checked the departures board again and sighed; his flight was going to be two hours late taking off. Air India, Zurich-Delhi-Bangalore. It was the third time he'd made this trip in the past six months, and the thrill of these long intercontinental flights was long gone, especially since flying business class was out of the question.

At least this time he had something special to look forward to: In a week, his 20-year-old son, Peter, who was a college student in California, was going to join him. The university's summer vacation was just starting, and Peter would fly out to meet his father in Beijing. They were going to make a father-son trip they had been talking about for a long time: a visit to the Chinese Space Center in Xichang. If everything went as planned, they would be able to watch the launch of China's third moon shot.

But first he had work to do. As director of human resources for Bank Bärtobel, one of Switzerland's venerable private banks, Zimmermann was flying out to India, then China, to interview candidates for the position of account executive. More than 80 percent of the bank's clients were from those two countries, and Zimmermann was given the task of gradually replacing the traditionally Swiss client contact staff with qualified Indian and Chinese professionals, who would be based locally. They could more easily meet with clients, would understand the local environment better, and also would be able to speak their language.

Much had changed in the Swiss private banking world over the past 15 years. Even before 2010, Switzerland had already begun feeling pressure from the European Union and the United States to turn over account information about European and American clients, as they were suspected of using their Swiss accounts, shielded by Swiss banking secrecy laws, to avoid—or even evade—taxes in their home countries. In rapid-fire sequence, three events had happened in 2016 and 2017 that spelled the end of banking secrecy forever and, with it, the end of Switzerland's traditional banking prowess.

The first blow came when Greece, Italy, and Spain all defaulted on their euro debt on the same day in October 2016—now called "Black Wednesday." The technical reasons were complex, but the immediate consequence was a last-ditch effort to bail out the three economies by the only country that could do it: Germany. This failed. Now hemorrhaging money, Germany, led by a left-wing German government since the previous year, insisted that all bank accounts held by German citizens anywhere outside the country be repatriated within 60 days, upon penalty of five years in prison. At the same time, Germany demanded cooperation from the Swiss government. The Swiss responded to Germany that very few Germans still held accounts in the country but that they would do their best to cooperate. In private communications, the government began to pressure all the banks in the country to close German accounts or face sanctions.

No doubt some German account holders would have decided to ride out the storm and risk being caught and punished, but the second blow followed within days. The whistleblower website Wikileaks published the names, addresses, and detailed bank account information of 447,000 EU citizens who kept money in 15 different banks in Switzerland, about a third of them Germans. No one knew where the information had come from, but the impact was devastating. The European Union, needing and wanting "its" money, accused Switzerland of bad faith and passed a motion in Brussels to terminate all nonessential trade and cooperation agreements with the Swiss. Several Swiss citizens, most of whom had no connection to the banking industry at all, were detained at airports in Brussels, Frankfurt, Paris, Rome, and Athens, under suspicion of assisting tax evasion and assorted other vaguely worded misdeeds. All were released within hours, but the rumor quickly spread that Swiss travelers could expect to be harassed by EU authorities until the situation was resolved.

Switzerland reacted by ordering every bank in the country to close all accounts held by any entity with an EU address. Pandemonium ensued as Europeans withdrew their money; the share prices of the major Swiss financial institutions tumbled between 30 and 50 percent; and the Swiss stock market had its worst month in 75 years.

In accordance with the Swiss legal system, Swiss banking secrecy could be abolished only by a nationwide referendum. This was quickly organized, with the vote set to take place in June 2017. However, before this could happen, a third event struck, which hammered the final nail in the coffin of banking secrecy. Backed by a huge promotional campaign under the headline "Financial Information Wants to Be Free," Google, in collaboration with Wikileaks, launched a new service called "Google Wealth." This website and app essentially gave users real-time information on the net worth of more than 100 million people in Europe and America, including details of their mortgages and credit card debt, the makeup of their securities portfolios, and their bank account balances. It was not possible to manipulate the accounts or initiate any transactions, but the information was freely available—and accurate.

Financial privacy died that day. The referendum passed, with 63 percent of the Swiss population voting to officially end banking secrecy (since it had already ended in practice, anyway). Within days, EU and US clients withdrew hundreds of billions of euros and dollars from their Swiss accounts.

It took Swiss banks about five years to regain their footing after this series of knockout punches; three or four

banks quietly closed their doors, and there were also a dozen or so mergers. Most banks had little choice but to rebrand themselves as purely domestic investment advisors, offering no privacy or discretion whatsoever. Indeed, the Google Wealth site received a million visitors a day; many people used it to check their own data. It was remarkably up to date. The only thing Google didn't appear to know was how much cash was in your wallet or how much money your brother-in-law owed you. But people joked that Google was working on it.

However, even the effort to reposition themselves proved difficult for the remaining Swiss banks, as it resulted in a hugely oversupplied market. A shakeout was inevitable.

Hans Zimmermann's bank was one of the survivors. With an excellent reputation going back to the 1920s, it had built up a relatively small but stable client base in Asia over the previous two decades. The bank's executives knew it could survive by continuing to offer these clients traditional private banking services. Twenty years of strong economic growth in India and China, as well as a handful of other countries in the Far East, had created a large market for more sophisticated banking and investment services. Competition was fierce, though. Banks and brokerages from Switzerland, the United Kingdom, the United States, and France went head-to-head for business, often coming up against cunning clients who played them off against each other with great skill. What's more, Chinese banks were also active in this business now, although to local high-net-worth individuals, they didn't have as much prestige as the foreign banks did.

Bank Bärtobel's board had decided to make the institution more Asian. It was aggressively expanding its network of more than 30 branches, primarily in China and India. Zurich was merely the bank's back office; much of the investment work had been automated, based on an excellent new Indian-developed investment software program.

As a human resources professional, Hans Zimmermann had not been involved in this IT installation, but he had gotten to know the head of the project team quite well and was looking forward to visiting him and his

"The best private banks—not just Swiss institutions, but also British, French, and American banks active in wealth management—have their pick of top MBAs, economics, and law graduates from ranking universities all over the world."

— from the Scenario *King of the World*

"Most [Swiss private] banks had little choice but to rebrand themselves as purely domestic investment advisors, offering no privacy or discretion whatsoever."

— from the Scenario *Song of India*

wife in Bangalore. He would also be meeting their daughter, who had just completed her MBA at Stanford Business School and was working with a Chinese-funded venture capital firm with offices in Palo Alto, Shenzhen, and Bangalore. Zimmermann wondered if maybe he could persuade her to join the bank as a management trainee, perhaps as an assistant to the CEO. She had just the kind of profile the bank needed to ensure its Asian-dependent future.

SCENARIO: "KING OF THE WORLD"

Bouncing with energy, Mexico City native Alicia Ruiz strides smartly down the concourse at Heathrow Airport, eager to board her flight to Zurich where she will be interviewing for a job at Bank Bärtobel. In two months Alicia will be graduating with an MBA from Oxford's Saïd Business School, and she was excited to learn just a few days ago that the highly respected Swiss bank was interested enough in her application to invite her to Switzerland for a battery of interviews. Wealth management is a booming business, and competition for jobs in private banking is fierce among business school students. The best private banks—not just Swiss institutions, but also British, French, and American banks active in wealth management—have their pick of top MBAs, economics, and law graduates from ranking universities all over the world.

As for Alicia, with her excellent education, previous experience as a financial analyst, and her perfectly bilingual background (her father is Mexican and her mother Swiss), she has high hopes of becoming an account executive with a prestigious Swiss bank, responsible for acquiring new Mexican clients and advising them on the global investment opportunities the bank's experts are discovering and analyzing on practically a daily basis.

It is 2025: What a great time to be in this business! A veritable explosion in private wealth has been sustained for over a decade now, thanks to the global economic recovery that began in 2013–14. That's when the world's key economies, led by the United States, introduced comprehensive pension and entitlement reforms, made drastic cuts in government spending, and also significantly reduced corporate and personal incomes taxes. The political left protested that this would never work, that it would make "fat cats" even fatter. But in fact, the result has been a true across-the-board stimulus that turbocharged investment and hiring by businesses, fueling a decade-long period of strong economic growth, excellent employment levels, and robust wealth creation.

Despite the fact that tax rates were reduced, within two years governments were actually collecting substantially more tax revenues than before, thanks to the higher levels of economic activity and profits this strategy began to generate. And because spending levels were lower, deficits and debt both shrank. Regaining the confidence they had been lacking for several years, the world's stock markets took off. The Dow and other leading indexes all doubled within 18 months.

Since then, private banks and other companies looking after the financial needs of high-net-worth individuals have been riding high. In the past 10 years, Bank Bärtobel opened 25 offices all around the world. They are especially successful in the "Six New BRICs"—the three Baltic countries, Mexico, Morocco, and Turkey. These six countries have been the home of literally thousands of new hypernetworked technology start-ups, minting a new breed of millionaire. Often, these newly wealthy entrepreneurs are looking not only for professional assistance in building and maintaining a portfolio of financial instruments, but also for real estate, seeking properties to own on a global basis. To add depth to their ability to provide this kind of service to their clients, in 2018 Bank Bärtobel acquired Sotheby's International Realty.

The Swiss government and population, meanwhile, have expressed their support for the banking industry on several occasions. A referendum to abolish banking secrecy was soundly defeated in 2013, and another one in 2022, by an even bigger margin. The Swiss people see the banking industry, and especially private banking, as a source of pride and as an economic engine for the country. Thanks to the economic boom, pressure from the European Union to weaken Switzerland's banking secrecy policies has also dried up. When the tax coffers of most EU countries are being filled due to the prosperity within their borders, there is less concern about punishing Switzerland for its role in allowing EU citizens some financial privacy.

An interesting marketing development has been under way for the past few years, which Alicia wants to ask Bank Bärtobel about. A few companies with excellent global brands and marketing know-how have been leveraging their relationships with high-net-worth clients to help them manage their wealth. They don't offer financial services or advice themselves, but typically work with private banks. One of the first of these strategic alliances, successful now for the past eight or nine years, is between Mercedes-Benz and UBS. Pictet teamed up with LVMH, and the Rothschild Group formed an extensive alliance with Ferrari, Christie's, Four Seasons Hotels, and yacht builders Perini Navi.

Settling into her seat on the plane, Alicia opens today's *Financial Times* and spots an article that brings a smile to her lips: Bank Bärtobel has just been ranked among the top 10 companies to work for in Europe. Wow! She cannot wait to arrive in Zurich.

CHAPTER 3

CASE STUDIES: THE REAL WORLD

It would be easy to think of scenario planning as a tool that is mainly useful to planners and decision makers in the business world. Corporations are typically interested in getting a handle on issues such as how consumer tastes and attitudes might develop, or how receptive markets might be to their new product ideas. So it would be natural to assume that such organizations are the main beneficiaries of scenario planning.

But this is shortchanging the potential value of the technique to so many other kinds of organizations, which can also use scenario planning to peer into the future and explore the alternative environments where, perhaps measuring success in different terms, they need to be every bit as effective as a business that is aiming to grow its market share or profits.

In the following part of the book, you'll find four case studies illustrating how different types of organizations have used scenario planning to visualize the way their future landscape might develop. In each case, they undertook the exercise to generate insights about the opportunities and threats that would be likely to emerge in a key area of activity so that they could take the necessary steps today to prepare themselves for the potential changes afoot.

To show that scenario planning benefits many outfits besides for-profit businesses, I've intentionally chosen some unusual practitioners:

- **The World Association of Newspapers** wanted to help its members understand how growing competition from new technologies and changing reading habits could create a new landscape for a product that has existed for centuries: the newspaper.

- **VisitScotland** wanted to be ready to accommodate changing patterns of world tourism and to find the best ways to attract tourists to their fair country.

- The **National Industries Corporation** of a well-known island republic wanted to evaluate how trends such as regional and global trade could have an impact on its mission to ensure the smooth development of the country's economy.

- Working with the **World Bank**, the **government of India** needed to understand how different scenarios for the social and economic climate in 2030 could improve decisions made today on large-scale agricultural reforms.

Some of these case studies describe scenario planning exercises that took place a few years ago. In those instances, we already have some idea which "future" is actually materializing now, and with the miracle of 20/20 hindsight, we can see how the planners may have missed certain developments that turned out to be important. But we can also see how prescient some of the scenarios were, mapping out a "big picture" that comes close to what is actually transpiring, even if a few of the details are wrong.

When reading these vignettes, cast your mind back to the time when the exercise was taking place and try to ignore what you might know has happened in the meantime. The participants in these sessions didn't know what we know now. They were striving to imagine what *could* materialize, and the case studies will be more instructive if you keep that in mind.

You'll note also that, other than government entities, there aren't any actual corporations among these case write-ups! There's a simple reason for that. Most companies consider the scenarios they develop as an important aspect of their strategic plans—in other words, they're highly confidential, not something to be splashed all over the pages of a book where their competitors could see them.

Last, bear in mind as well that these case write-ups cannot hope to be anything more than hugely simplified summaries of the in-depth scenario planning processes that these various organizations went through, in some cases involving dozens of people and stretching over several months. I apologize to the many players involved for having to condense and abridge their fascinating thinking processes, insights, and narratives down to just a few pages. Obviously, by doing this I've had to leave out a lot of details that make these stories so interesting, but I've made every effort to give you a sense of how their workshops and discussions proceeded, step by thought-provoking step. . . and wherever possible, I've also tried to include the juiciest of the juicy bits!

Case Study: The Newspaper Industry

RADICAL TRANSFORMATION: SINK OR SWIM?

The dissemination of written news has been around for a very long time. It appears to have begun in Roman times as a way for government officials to communicate, mostly with each other, but also for occasional announcements to the masses ("Glorious Victory in Latest Battle, details on tablet 4").

At first, these bulletins were not printed, of course. Julius Caesar carved the news on stone. In China during the Han Dynasty, around the year AD 200, official notices were handwritten on silk.

Manually produced notices were the rule of the day for centuries, severely limiting distribution. Then Gutenberg invented movable type in the mid-1400s. Even so, however, it still took another 100 years, until the 1550s, for the Republic of Venice to publish the first *avviso*—something we would recognize today as a newspaper. By the 1700s these news broadsheets were being published all across Europe and in the major cities of North America, and about a century later, thanks to Western influence, newspapers finally came to the Far East as well.

WHERE WE ARE TODAY

Today there are some 6,000 daily newspapers published all over the world, reaching an audience of 400 million every day. Counting weeklies, the number is still higher.

Sounds like a great success story, doesn't it? However, these numbers belie the fact that the newspaper industry now faces a critical period of transition. In the developed world, the industry's three main revenue pillars—paid circulation (i.e., subscriptions), newsstand sales, and the most important of the three, advertising—are declining, and because of that, profitability at many publishing companies is under severe pressure. Clearly, some won't survive.

How did the decline come about? Newspaper publishers lived through the advent of radio and television just fine. But beginning in the 1990s, they first encountered a new kind of competitor: round-the-clock news channels on cable TV. These began to chip away at newspapers' circulation, and what began as a slow erosion became a landslide once the Internet took off and readers abandoned paying for newspapers, turning instead to free online news. Lower circulation numbers meant that ad rates had to be lowered, squeezing profits further. Newspaper companies responded in various ways: laying off staff, cutting salaries, or reducing their publishing frequency, for example. Some simply put themselves up for sale, though valuations had plummeted. A few folded. Others are still busy trying to reinvent themselves using mobile, video, and social media, with mixed results.

Conversely, in the developing world, cheap newsprint and lower distribution costs, coupled with a growing middle class, increased literacy, and limited access to the Internet, have ensured that newspapers are actually doing well. In India, for instance, revenues are growing 15 percent a year.

So, it is in the industrialized countries that the industry is in peril. The number of newspapers that have actually gone out of business in the past few years because of their inability to sustain losses (or is it because of an inability to adapt to a new business model?) has been alarming. The website www.newspaperdeathwatch.com (whose name alone gives you some idea of the grim situation) lists a dozen large metropolitan dailies that have closed in the United States since 2007, and eight more that have switched to online or hybrid models. Venerable names such as the *Rocky Mountain News*, *Seattle Post-Intelligencer*, and *Honolulu Advertiser* are gone; the *Christian Science Monitor* and *Detroit News/Free Press* have been severely scaled back as print publications. In addition, more than 150 others have closed, many of them nondailies that struggled during the past decade and were then finished off by the economic downturn starting in 2008.

ENTER SCENARIO PLANNING

The World Association of Newspapers and News Publishers (WAN-IFRA) is the global organization of the world's newspapers, with its head office in Paris. Its mission encompasses lofty goals such as promoting freedom of the press and quality journalism, but it also considers as one of its core objectives to help the industry's players develop prosperously. And that, WAN-IFRA saw, was definitely not happening.

In 2007, recognizing the increasing degree of pain that the industry was going through (and would likely continue to experience for some time), WAN-IFRA decided to try to get a handle on the way the newspaper business could develop, looking out to the year 2020.

"In 2007, the media industry was—and still is—in transformation," says Larry Kilman, the organization's deputy CEO. "There's constant flux, primarily due to new digital media platforms. Unfortunately, forecasts and predictions about the future have been all over the map. So we decided to take an informed, scenario planning approach to understanding how the future landscape might look in 2020."

Larry and his team briefed the Stockholm-based consulting firm Kairos Future on their need to see the alternatives that lay ahead, and Kairos jumped into action, planning a two-day workshop in January 2008 that would eventually involve 19 newspaper executives from 15 different countries.

GROUNDWORK

But first, there was homework to do. Wanting to paint a broad picture of the challenges facing the industry worldwide and produce a map of the emerging competitive and consumer trends and their web of uncertainties, Kairos conducted interviews with a select number of CEOs and COOs in the newspaper business, ranging from *Aftenposten* in Oslo and Fairfax Media in

Australia to the *New York Times*. They asked these industry leaders a range of questions, some general and others industry-specific. For example:

General

If you could look into the future, what would you like to know?

If the future unfolded according to your wishes, realistically but optimistically, what would it look like?

If the future unfolded in the wrong direction, what would you worry about?

Specific

What kind of content will newspapers contain in 2020, and how will this differ from content in 2007?

What three major changes need to happen in order for the newspaper industry to be successful in 2020?

How will newspaper revenue sources change between 2007 and 2020?

Who are newspapers' competitors in 2020 compared with 2007, and how do newspapers compete with them?

What role do newspapers play in society in 2020 compared with 2007?

Based on these one-on-one dialogues, as well as additional research conducted on their own, Kairos came up with an extensive list of 66 trends (which they termed "uncertainties") that appeared to be shaping the newspaper business as 2007 ticked over to 2008.

Then came the scenario planning workshop itself. To help stimulate the discussion among the larger group of participants, this long list of 66 trends was picked over, discussed, argued about, and then eventually ranked in importance.

By casting their votes for the trends they thought were the most important, the 19 members of the group chose the following as the most important issues needing to be addressed over the coming decade:

1. New revenue models

Not surprisingly, the senior executives from the industry found that the number one issue they needed to face was developing new models. Technology could enable this, they felt, and listed a number of tech-based ideas that could become key elements in a new newspaper model, such as rich-media ads, product placement, maglogs, and even virtual worlds.

2. Multichannel strategies

Linked with the preceding top-ranked uncertainty, the participants also saw a future where there would be less distinction between newspapers, TV, radio, and the Web. A newspaper company may have to be present in all of these channels.

3. User-generated content

With people increasingly creating and sharing their own news and opinions, newspapers might need to accommodate this new development in some way. This also means that newspapers could become platforms for social interaction.

4. Shifting importance from channel to content

Simply, consumers were beginning to consider content more important than the channel where they found it. That would mean that newspapers would need to choose to make use of the most appropriate channel for the type of content they would be disseminating.

5. Target market segmentation

Since choice and access were expanding, customers would have greater freedom to select what interested them most. Newspapers might have to focus their editorial concepts and target specific segments.

6. More mobile broadband

There would be a proliferation of WiFi-enabled mobile devices, and they would get smaller, faster, and more user-friendly.

7. Simplifying your life

Self-explanatory, no? Newspaper customers will be more attracted to what's easy and tend to avoid what's complicated.

8. Audience fragmentation

This final top-rated trend is implied by the increasing proliferation of both channels and content; namely, the audience for any given channel and content would be thinning out as the mass market splinters into its subsegments following only particular topics.

Also receiving votes, but not deemed quite as critical as the preceding items, were the trend toward hyperlocal newspapers, for example, and the uncertainty about whether online-only companies might become newspaper competitors.

Clearly, some of these trends were interrelated, so the group next mapped out cause-and-effect linkages. What began to take shape then was a still-wooly notion of the chain of causality that different trends might bring about (i.e., the first hint of certain patterns that might emerge). Some important details were still missing, though. For example, how fast could some of these developments come to pass? In other words, how quickly might the newspapers have to move?

In addition to the top-ranked trends, it is also interesting to look at some of the trends that the group did *not* consider to be as critical as the ones they did choose. For example, most of the specifically technological trends fielded among the original list of 66 didn't seem to impress the group so much as potential game changers for the future, including:

- Digital printing
- Intelligent paper
- E-paper (i.e., foldable displays)
- Higher print quality
- Location-based media (in which GPS enables localized content and ads)
- Greater video content (i.e., a move toward visual communication)
- Push services/RSS
- Improved measurement and monitoring made possible by digital media

Likewise, other than the trend toward a simpler lifestyle, most demographic or societal uncertainties that were included in the 66 also failed to make the final cut. Among them:

- Gray panthers (i.e., older but richer customers)
- Increased individualism
- Less loyalty, more "grazing"
- New family constellations
- Just-in-time living (i.e., lack of time)
- Increasingly "professional" customers who better understood the competitive options and prices available
- Greater choice across a spectrum of consumers' lives

CREATING SCENARIOS

The next step in the process was to develop a scenario cross, as we've seen in Chapter 2. At the WAN-IFRA workshop, the Kairos consultants broke the group into small teams and asked each one to have a go at defining the axes that might best reflect the major uncertainties in the business environment. In each case, the idea was to define an either/or pair; both outcomes should be plausible.

After discussing the teams' suggestions, the group settled on these two issues, both of which referred to enormous, but not yet settled, possibilities that would affect any newspaper company's competitiveness.

Why These Pairings?

Mass audience versus targeted audiences. If you look at newspapers from a historical perspective, their mission has almost always been to address the information needs of a mass audience. For example, you target everyone living in Cedar Rapids, not just the veterinarians living there. The issue for the group to ponder, therefore, was whether this would continue to be the case in the future. As the mass market splinters, with self-selecting groups beginning to focus on specific themes, and as it becomes easier for people to find information that interests them—sourced from anywhere on earth—could a case be made that the future belongs to the newspapers that, for example, cater specifically to the veterinarians of Cedar Rapids instead of all the city's citizens?

Dominance of traditional media versus disruptive media. Looking at the other pair of alternatives, newspapers have by and large existed in their present form for centuries, and during all that time they have been true to one medium, the printed page. These printed pages are physically distributed to readers who may each have their own preferred way of consuming a newspaper but who cannot get around the physical necessity of handling it and reading it as a paper product. Disruptive media, on the other hand, are all those nonprint formats—delivered online via a number of possible devices or channels—that could come along and upset the apple cart. In 2020, will the newspaper business continue to be dominated by these traditional print media, or will online media have taken the lead, consumers having grown to prefer this new way to get and read the news?

Combining these two pairs into a scenario cross, Kairos now had the framework that would allow them and the group to imagine how four very different futures could play out.

The group then spent their remaining time together fleshing out how the scenarios would look and feel as actual business landscapes. What would society be like? What about consumer attitudes and preferences? What would the role of changing technology be in each of the four scenarios? Who would be the most formidable competitors?

They tackled this imaginative task by pretending it was already the year 2020, and from that future vantage point, they crafted four stories to explain "retroactively" how each particular scenario would have emerged over the 12 years between 2008 and 2020.

As with all scenario planning, the key was not to restrict their imagined world to the future of the newspaper industry alone (that was too narrow a view), but to try and see how demographics, society's attitudes, technology, and many other factors might all interact to give each of the four distinct competitive environments a unique look and feel.

The four basic scenarios were discussed, and ideas hashed out, big and small, regarding what that world would be like. Then over the following few days, the Kairos consultants worked closely with WAN-IFRA to expand and fine-tune these basic notions, resulting in four detail-rich vignettes.

Let's look at the four scenarios in turn, beginning with the upper-right quadrant of the matrix.

Disruptive media dominates

Mass audience

Targeted audiences

Traditional media dominates

SCENARIO: "DISRUPTIVE MEDIA DOMINATE + TARGETED AUDIENCES"

Cleverly borrowing from the James Bond oeuvre to name the four scenarios, Kairos calls this future **"For Your Eyes Only."**

"The printed page. . . is rapidly nearing extinction," this scenario description begins, going straight for the jugular. The go-to medium in 2020, to nobody's surprise, is the Internet. There are still a few stragglers in the ink-smeared-on-dead-trees world, but most news organizations (nobody calls themselves "newspapers" anymore) have moved online.

Because a website is a globally accessible medium, competition between these companies has become fierce, not just for readers based on their location, but also in terms of content. Niche has become the name of the game, with narrowly focused news providers vying with each other to be the dominant provider of news on a particular topic. Mass media are all but gone. Accordingly, journalists are not mere reporters anymore but actual experts on their subject. Most are freelancers. The news and information they provide is very focused and high-quality.

Without print editions to produce, the barriers to entry in this landscape are low, so new entrants abound. At the same time, though, the giants of this world (Google, Microsoft, etc.) have the resources to launch new services and apps practically every day. That is hard to keep up with, and the group surmised that no traditional newspaper has a website in 2020 that ranks in the world's top 50.

To some extent, this scenario has come about because a new generation of readers grew up in the decade from 2010 to 2020—and for these young people, technology was like mother's milk. What's more, these young folks have a different attitude toward sharing their personal data. They're willing to give up information about themselves in exchange for an assurance that the stream of news and information, ads and entertainment that they receive continues to be relevant to them socially but also highly selective and tailored for their specific interests. This means that advertising is also highly targeted toward specific profiles—and, because it is more effective, it costs more.

In 2020, readers set up their own portals—a "Daily Me" of feeds corresponding to their highly specific information wishes, which also serve as targeted ad platforms. New services such as "Google Grid" become hubs for people to store and share media; in addition, "the Grid" ranks and sorts news based on what a user's online "friends" are viewing. Comments are possible on everything in this hyperfragmented world. User-generated content is increasingly important, too, and on some sites, models will be in place that actually pay people a split of the revenues generated by their online contributions.

In this scenario, handheld devices allowing consumers to get news on the go will proliferate—but it won't be just news that people are after but also information that is geotagged (i.e., location-specific). Examples the group came up with: Standing outside a movie theater, you can watch trailers for the movies being shown; outside a restaurant, you can pull down the menu or see a live feed of the establishment—and all garnished with other users' opinions and reviews. Sound messy? One positive outcome is that, in general, businesses put more emphasis on the quality of their products and services than before. How could they risk not doing this, when their customers are pumping out ratings and reviews 24/7?

In this world, newspaper publishers repeatedly downsize and reorganize in their struggle to keep up with the more agile, faster-moving digital media. They also find it difficult to recruit talent, and this has hurt them as well.

The group sums up this scenario: "Newspapers are common only among the elite and the elderly." Otherwise, the old media world has changed beyond recognition.

SCENARIO: "TRADITIONAL MEDIA DOMINATE + TARGETED AUDIENCES"

"Diamonds Are Forever" is the name of the second scenario, reflecting the fact that newspapers are still around in 2020 and thriving. Considered by consumers as a vital part of their culture, newspapers are still enjoying their long tradition of quality and trustworthiness, coexisting comfortably with TV, radio, and the Internet.

Indeed, it's this long history, and the credibility they've built up over many years, that's protecting them from otherwise stiff competition online. The proliferation of more and more information sources on the Web (can you really trust them?) only serves to reinforce the need people feel for news that has been properly gathered, written, and vetted and that appears in an established medium with a name they trust.

"Credibility will be the keyword to success and to companies' endurance," said Nelson Sirotsky, the CEO of Brazil's Grupo RBS and a workshop participant. "We must consider that on the one hand, the new platforms have democratized the information production and distribution process, but on the other hand, they have created an avalanche of contents and a great mixture of good and bad things."

Readers' confidence in new digital news providers took a hit when a number of scandals during the 2010s revealed how they put profits ahead of ethical standards. Consequently, over the past decade, there's been a classic flight to quality.

But that doesn't mean there haven't been any changes in the landscape. For one thing, newspapers did branch out into other media, but under the same brand umbrella there is now a blurring of the distinctions between newspapers, TV, radio, and the Web, since text, images, audio, and video are all used in combination where it makes the most sense. Content is more important than channel, and newspapers see themselves as "news organizations," no longer tied to a single medium.

At the same time, increased individualism, especially on the part of younger readers, means that media cater to niche interests more and more. Online, this has led to a wave of acquisitions as the media groups bought up existing specialist sites rather than trying to build up their own. Following this industry consolidation, the big media groups now boast portfolios of brands, each addressing specific reader interests. Cross-promotion among sites in the same family keeps visitors within the bundle.

The niche approach means consumers are happier with the content they receive, since it corresponds more closely with their own interests. Those willing to share personal data get ads for products and services that are linked to their interests and profile, too. In general, the media groups are more sensitive to what consumers want.

What also emerged over the 2008 to 2020 period was an understanding that people liked reading newspapers for in-depth reporting, but in addition they wanted to receive brief snippets of news and updates delivered electronically over the course of the day. The "killer app" that came along during this period consisted of short local TV loops broadcast not only to television and the Web, but also to smartphones. Local blogs, TV, and newspapers covered local events, gave comments and opinions, and could put a local spin on global or national news. News went hyperlocal.

Local papers saw this as a stepping-stone to transforming their sites into platforms filled with locally oriented content generated in part by users such as local interest groups, associations, clubs, and the like. Communities form around these information posts. This in turn attracts local advertisers with goods and services to offer to those specific profiles. Local papers have built on this new dynamism to become experts in search engine optimization, sharing ad revenues with content generators, and becoming de facto media brokers.

Last, digital printing makes print-on-demand versions of newspapers possible, which is necessary now that environmental regulations restrict the "transportation of unnecessary goods" in order to save energy.

SCENARIO: "TRADITIONAL MEDIA DOMINATE + MASS AUDIENCE"

This scenario is based on the idea that over the decade leading to 2020, consumers felt they were being flooded with online information, much of it sensationalistic and, bottom line, untrustworthy. So they have been returning instead to the old tried-and-true media: newspapers. Here, they know that what they're getting is solid, reliable news and information.

To bolster this relationship with their consumers and to take advantage of their need for authenticity, newspaper companies in 2020 have been investing in brand building to strengthen their image of credibility. The happy result: "Newspapers have managed to become almost indispensable for the majority."

Another factor that has helped newspapers in this scenario is the increasingly time-starved consumer, who doesn't want to waste valuable time sifting through all the information bombarding him or her every day on the Internet. Online ads are a big part of this flood of unwanted info, and many people have resorted to ad-blocking software to filter it out. Great for them, but not so great for the advertisers. Consequently, print advertising in newspapers has begun to look attractive to them again: After all, it's unblockable!

Not everything is unicorns and rainbows in this world, however. Circulations are still falling, not so much because readers are abandoning newspapers for the Internet, but because newspapers have had to redefine what they do better compared to online media, and this has resulted in an editorial shift to more analysis and less news. News in fact has become something of a commodity. This shift toward offering context and increased in-depth writing has meant that newspapers need to specialize in certain subject areas more than before (e.g., on politics or sports or entertainment) rather than trying to be all things to all people. The upside has been stronger, more appreciated brands, sometimes even tied to individual personalities on the writing staff. But since the newspapers appeal to a narrower segment of the reading population, circulation is lower. Some newspapers have responded to this pressure by trying to make their news not just informative but more entertaining, too. That has led to some navel-gazing in the industry about the real role of a news organization.

One path to boost circulation that has been tried is to offer the newspaper for free, charging only a modest fee for home delivery. This has worked in a few cases. But the editorial changes most papers are going through usually mean that the newspaper itself is of higher quality (printing, graphics, etc.) and therefore more expensive to produce. Giving it away for free may not always be a sensible thing to do.

In this scenario, personalization hasn't taken off, mainly because people are still reluctant to submit personal data about themselves. This means that publishers aren't able to customize their product too much based on reader profiles.

The Kairos consultants gave this scenario the name **"Die Another Day."** Newspapers have survived and, given a more focused strategy, they look set to continue to do so. For the time being at least, all is well.

SCENARIO: "DISRUPTIVE MEDIA DOMINATE + MASS AUDIENCE"

"Thunderball," with its imagery of a giant, explosive finale, is the last of the four 2020 scenarios: The Internet wins. People go online for everything media-related: news, entertainment, sports, analysis, opinion, TV, movies, music, radio, games. This convergence is so dramatic that the key players, offering all these services on an integrated platform, are also the providers of choice of social media. Google, Microsoft, and NBS (a new integrated communication company postulated by Kairos) are the media giants of 2020.

Demand for news has proven to be more of a one-size-fits-all approach after all, and, particularly, young consumers tend to hang out at a site, reading news, watching videos, and interactively partaking of different services together with their friends—in essence creating both the news-consuming experience as well as the content.

Newspapers, interestingly, are not dead—far from it. However, they are published by Google, for example, forming just one of the myriad communication channels that this giant controls. Some are user-generated; some are financed through the company's very efficient ad-space auctions. Google offers advertisers advanced and quite accurate measurement tools, even for print ads, meaning that advertisers pay only for results.

Speaking of user-generated content, online news is also produced and edited collaboratively, for example on Wikipedia 2.0. Here, users contribute text, images, and casual video, interviews, map data, expert analysis, and comments, and a system has been put into place to ensure authenticity.

Driving these developments have been a number of exciting technological advances. Handheld devices in 2020 are light, thin, and cheap. For example, Apple launched iPaper, a foldable display allowing the user to read the news, get updates, watch TV, and view movies. Thanks partly to such

devices, news has morphed into a more visual mode, even 3D. And in the ambient environment, displays are everywhere, offering news and public information, often location-based.

At the same time, the Internet is closely linked to the physical world in the sense that most products, not to mention ads and TV programs, have their own websites, and smartphones and other mobile devices have become "sniffer tools," reading bar codes and other tags to link to them directly for additional information, opinion, and so on.

Newspapers have a hard time fitting in in this world. One option seems to be to fall back on their know-how as news gatherers and provide unique content as subcontractors to Google and NBS and the other giants. But this doesn't help their brand and ultimately makes it hard for them to attract talent, both on the journalistic side and commercial side of the business. Another route to potential success would be to focus on a narrow niche, but can advertising support it? Or a final option: Sell out to an Internet giant, signing over the news staff to that company and getting out of the business.

Now What?

As they should, the four scenarios (and remember, these are merely summaries!) present quite different views of how 2020 might look. The CEOs and strategists now have the challenge of preparing their companies for not one of these scenarios, but potentially all four.

HOW WELL DID THEY DO?

The scenario planning workshop you've just read about took place in January 2008—not all that long ago, but with the accelerated pace of technological change, which is clearly driving many of the trends affecting the newspaper business, a lot can happen in four or five short years.

Indeed, a very big change did come along in this period. The workshop participants postulated that by 2020, some kind of new light handheld devices could be game changers for the industry. In reality, it didn't take that long. In 2010, Apple launched the iPad, just 27 months after the workshop had imagined that an iPad-like device could become an important factor in the future of the business.

Score one for the group. The larger question, however, is this: Does the advent of the iPad and its rival devices signal to the newspaper industry that scenario 1 or scenario 4 (i.e., the dominance of disruptive media) is emerging?

Or is the iPad merely a reading tool that still needs content—something news organizations are uniquely qualified to supply? Has the iPad therefore given newspaper publishers a fantastic new opportunity to gear their content to this new medium? To put it all another way, is it *paper* that makes a newspaper a newspaper? Or is it *news*?

Four years on, it would seem that publishers have come to the conclusion that controlling the channel is less important than controlling the content. They are keen to give readers whatever format they want now, so they are making content available in the form of apps and e-books—whatever the next big new thing happens to be. In short, publishers want to enhance the reader experience—a phrase that didn't emerge in the workshop. The format is part of that experience, but it isn't all of it. Content is still critical.

In another area, the workshop also proved to be good at foreseeing the outcome of important trends. Location-based apps such as Foursquare and Gowalla are just a step away from the feature mentioned in scenario 1, in which we can pass by a restaurant and instantly receive the menu on our phones. Right now, instead of the menu, what we can get is a coupon from the restaurant, as well as other people's ratings and reviews. But the day is surely coming.

Which brings us to the one thing that the workshop apparently didn't foresee so clearly: the rise of social media and its impact. Facebook was mentioned, for example, but its pervasiveness in every nook and cranny of young people's lives wasn't understood at that point. Although some of the scenarios posited by the WAN-IFRA group counted on the fact that in 2020, people would be happy to share their personal data, in reality, thanks to Facebook and Twitter we are already in a world today where communities are established in hours through shared data, opinions, and observations.

For sure, some of these observations encroach on what a newspaper might ordinarily think of as its turf. The 2011 political upheavals in North Africa were fueled by observations posted to Twitter by eyewitnesses. We're already seeing more and more examples of people turning reflexively to Twitter for breaking news rather than traditional news outlets. Tweets may lack accuracy or professionalism, but their immediacy cannot be overlooked!

Extra! Extra!
Tweet all about it!

Case Study: The National Industries Corporation

CHARTING A COURSE FOR ECONOMIC DEVELOPMENT

Strewn over dozens of islands in a 50-mile-long chain, the tiny Republic we will take a look at now is one of the world's smallest countries, both in land area and population. It's also one of the planet's lowest countries: With an average altitude (if that's the right word) of just 4 feet 11 inches (1.5 meters) above sea level, the country has become a focus for climate change concerns. Rising sea levels, so go the doomsayers' prognostications, will swamp the entire country unless the global warming trend is reversed.

In the meantime, the country's economy is largely dependent on just two industries: *tourism*, which accounts for 20 percent of the nation's GDP but brings in about 90 percent of its tax revenues, and *tuna fishing*.

THE NATIONAL INDUSTRIES CORPORATION

Until just 50 years ago, the Republic was not only one of the earth's lowest countries, but also one of the most isolated on the planet. Its tiny population of 100,000 could communicate with the outside world only by Morse code and ham radio. The country's only airport was an old Emergency Services airstrip, and transportation between the islands was limited to long trips on slow boats. The country's banking system was rudimentary, and investment in the country was practically zero. Everything but fish had to be imported, so prices were high even for everyday items.

It was, in short, a very backward place, and its future didn't look like it would improve any time soon.

Recognizing the pressing need for an efficient central purchasing organization that could help raise the Republic's living standards and encourage development, the country established a trading agency in the 1960s, which expanded a short while later into the company known today as the National Industries Corporation (NIC). Its original mission was to ensure the supply of a variety of wholesale and retail products imported from abroad, such as fuel, staple foods, construction materials, and pharmaceuticals, and to keep prices stable in the local economy.

Over time, the country did develop, with international tourism transforming the Republic into a sun worshipper's paradise and generating lots of earnings for the country's coffers. As the standard of living improved, the NIC's mission grew as well. It began to focus not only on basic goods and services, but also moved upmarket, importing higher-quality merchandise and state-of-the-art consumer products.

Today, the NIC's role is to help broaden the country's sources of revenue. It has become the parent company of a number of diversified subsidiaries and joint ventures in sectors such as oil and gas, cement, roofing materials, and even insurance services. Its sights are set still higher. According to the NIC website, the company aims to be a diverse multinational in the future, the first company in the Republic to be listed on an internationally recognized stock exchange. "We plan investment in local manufacturing," it says, "and wish to be recognized as a leader in innovation." A laudable goal, but what will the future have to be like in order for the NIC to achieve it?

WHAT ABOUT THE FUTURE?

In the late 2000s, the NIC decided to find out. In the process of putting together a long-term strategic plan, the company specifically wanted to explore the way forward for attracting investment to the Republic, particularly in hospitality (the country's major breadwinner) and in various other domestic industries. In addition, each of NIC's main business areas was facing increasing competition from private (i.e., not state-owned) companies based in the Republic, and the NIC wanted to improve its market position for the future.

To help NIC understand how the future might unfold, and identify its opportunities and threats, executives called in Amplios, a Singapore-based consulting firm, who recommended conducting a scenario planning exercise that would then provide inputs to a strategic plan.

In 2008, the Amplios team got under way. One of the team's first tasks was to help NIC senior executives identify the driving forces that they believed would shape the Republic's economy in the next decade. After a long list had been developed and discussed, the planning team grouped them into a number of clusters.

Two of these clusters were named "Tourism Export Earnings" and "Fishing Export Earnings," reflecting the important impact that the health of the country's two main industries would have on the islanders' well-being. "Hospitality success is mission critical to the future of the Republic," said Wilson Fyffe, Amplios's president director and head of the project team. "So with our scenarios, we had to be sure to evaluate the likely business environment for international tourism and long-haul travel."

Other clusters assembled structural or environmental factors that could change the country's business climate. For example, how would trends in "Aviation" and "Shipping" affect the Republic? How would "Real Estate Development" play out? How could the "Domestic Business" environment and local "Political Development" shape NIC's competitiveness? Was there scope for the Republic to become a "Global Tech Center"?

"Quality of Life" issues were also raised, especially the availability of food and fuel. And the country's overall "Self-Sufficiency" was a cluster, too.

Last, looming over all the others was another cluster: "Climate Change."

CREATING BASIC SCENARIOS

Before fleshing out the details of how the actual future scenarios might look and feel, a pair of variables was needed to create a scenario cross. The participants decided that the key dimensions differentiating the alternative futures were "GDP Growth" (either high or low) and "Balance of Trade" (i.e., the volume and dynamism of the Republic's international commerce), also either high or low.

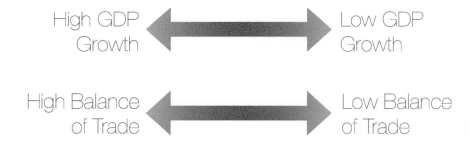

High GDP Growth ⟷ Low GDP Growth

High Balance of Trade ⟷ Low Balance of Trade

With these variables as the axes, the Amplios consulting team created a matrix with four quadrants, naming each one to reflect the positioning that would result for the Republic in that particular scenario:

The four scenarios were characterized in enormous detail (too much to repeat here, in fact). But you can get an idea of the depth of the thinking that went into the scenarios from the following excerpts from Amplios' report.

What we see for each scenario is that the team conjectured a large number of future events or milestones that each pertain to the 11 clusters they'd defined in their preliminary discussions. For example, all four scenarios include a description of what the future landscape looks like from the point of view of real estate development in the islands, aviation, and so on—as you'd expect, the situation for these clusters differs from one scenario to another, sometimes only in degree, but sometimes more fundamentally.

Next, we'll use scenario 1 ("Global Winner") as the baseline for our summary, as two of the others ("Global Trader" and "Regional Player") are essentially variations on this theme. However, the fourth scenario, "Safe Refuge," is very different—dark days ahead.

High GDP Growth

Global Trader

Global Winner

Low Balance of Trade

High Balance of Trade

Safe Refuge

Regional Player

Low GDP Growth

SCENARIO: "GLOBAL WINNER" (HIGH GDP GROWTH + HIGH BALANCE OF TRADE)

In this scenario, as you can tell from its name, the Republic is reaping the success from a high-growth, high-trade future. Amplios postulated that some of the outcomes this scenario would generate for the country include the following points. The NIC would find these elements to its advantage.

Economic/business development landscape

- The government has paid down its external debt so that servicing it can be done more sustainably. To do this, some state-owned enterprises have been sold off.
- Inflation is under 6 percent.
- The country's legal system has been brought up to international standards, which has been a boon to foreign direct investment.
- A business incubator now exists in the Republic.
- Domestic transport and logistics have received needed investment.
- Over 15,000 new jobs have been created outside the capital city.

Quality of life

- Electricity is available to every household in the Republic 24 hours per day.
- Regular ferry services now ply the waters between the islands, and public transportation has improved in the outlying islands.
- Pensions for the elderly have been made possible, partly financed by a new corporate and personal tax but partly by the international retirement home industry.
- All essential medicines are available to 100 percent of the population through the government's medical insurance plan.
- Thanks to the substantial improvements in the domestic economy, there's been a big increase in the number of citizens of the Republic returning home who had previously emigrated.

Aviation

- British Airways has introduced a budget service to the capital city, which supports the development of three-star tourism on this main island, providing a variation to tourists who are in four- and five-star accommodations on the other islands.
- Investments have been made in new airport facilities; the international airport's cargo terminal has been upgraded; and airport ground handling has been improved.

Shipping

- In the main harbors, a big investment in bunkering facilities has been made; dredging projects are under way; and the container yard has been upgraded.
- An entire cluster of ports and logistics companies has sprung up.
- To cut the costs of interisland freight services, a fleet of catamarans has been put in service.

Climate change

- The Republic gets 10 percent of its energy from nonpolluting sources.
- Battery-powered vehicles have replaced cars with internal combustion engines.
- Building codes have been changed so the main population centers won't be affected by a rise in sea levels of even one meter.

Fishing export earnings

- Ornamental fish farms have been established for the international aquarium trade.

Self-sufficiency

- Rooftop hydroponic farming has improved self-sufficiency in agricultural produce; the agriculture sector's contribution to GDP has gone up to 5 percent.
- Local growing initiatives have replaced half a dozen items that were previously imported.
- A company based in the Republic has made a major investment in a wheat farm in Canada to ensure supply of wheat to the country.

Tourism export earnings

- There have been no major international flare-ups, no terrorist activities, and no natural disasters affecting the long-haul tourist trade from Europe, North America and Asia.
- Oil prices have continued to rise, but there hasn't been any substantial impact on the four- and five-star resort trade.
- The Republic has maintained its standing as one of the most popular long-haul destinations in the coral reef segment.
- Sanitation has been improved throughout the country, particularly in the tourist resort areas.
- The Republic has successfully branded itself as a luxurious business conference destination.
- In the capital city, a tourist aquarium has been opened for visitors who don't dive themselves.

SCENARIO: "GLOBAL TRADER" (HIGH GDP GROWTH + LOW BALANCE OF TRADE)

The key difference between this scenario and the previous one is the lower level of the Republic's international commerce, particularly tourism. This has a knock-on effect throughout the economy.

Here are the key elements of this scenario that are different from the "Global Winner" scenario:

Economic/business development landscape

- Investment in tourism infrastructure is still encouraged, but with the slowdown in international tourist travel, these investments are underperforming.

Tourism export earnings

- International tensions, the lack of resolution of the major causes of terrorism, and even some natural disasters have all had a negative impact on the long-haul tourist trade.
- Rising oil prices (i.e., more expensive long-haul flights) have also contributed to the decline in four- and five-star resort bookings, resulting in underutilization of the resorts.
- Competition from other tropical coral reef destinations is growing, threatening the Republic's top ranking in this segment.
- The Republic has only been moderately successful in branding itself as a luxurious business conference destination.
- Aviation
- Despite their upgrade, the country's airports are also being underutilized, thanks to the lower number of international arrivals.

SCENARIO: "REGIONAL TRADER" (LOW GDP GROWTH + HIGH BALANCE OF TRADE)

This scenario differs from the "Global Winner" in a few critical areas:

Economic/business development landscape

- The lower levels of domestic business activity have a double-edged effect. On the one hand, local costs are low, so certain business opportunities are more attractive to international investors, and a commission has been set up to attract more foreign direct investment. On the other hand, consumers don't have the wherewithal to pay for certain high-cost services, so the government has to step in and subsidize various projects if it wants them to be realized. There is frequent resistance to fee structures proposed to finance the operation of some new infrastructure undertakings.
- Tax revenues are well below target levels.
- Because of the modest success of government programs, only 5,000 new jobs have been created outside the capital city.
- Conflict between expatriate blue-collar workers and locals has become an area of concern.
- The government's program to replace cars that have internal combustion engines with battery-powered vehicles has been successful, creating jobs and also benefiting the country's highly successful new three-star tourist trade.

Quality of life

- Electricity is available 24 hours a day to 80 percent of the households in the Republic.
- Ferry services exist between the islands, but the investment is moving ahead slowly, and fares have to be subsidized by the government.
- Pensions for the elderly are being provided, but the country's poor domestic economic performance means that corporate and personal tax revenues needed to finance them are below expectations.

- Thanks to the weak domestic economy, but high international trading status, skilled citizens are being offered attractive employment packages to relocate overseas. Shortage of skilled local technicians has made it difficult to go ahead with certain projects like the global tech center proposed in the "Global Winner" scenario.

Aviation

- Airport facilities are being improved, but investments are mainly being made in locations benefiting the tourist trade, not the local population.
- The British Airways budget service to the capital, launched to support the three-star tourist activity, has been very successful due to the fact that the depressed economy has kept costs low throughout the country.

SCENARIO: "SAFE REFUGE" (LOW GDP GROWTH + LOW BALANCE OF TRADE)

This is, relatively speaking, the doom-and-gloom scenario for the Republic's future. But it isn't as bad as all that. Even in this less-than-stellar future landscape, the government has built a global e-learning center, a telemedicine center operating at global best-practice standards, and several internationally recognized research centers. (These are all included in the other three scenarios as well.)

As before, long-haul travel has been affected by high oil prices, earthquakes, international unrest, and terrorism (the usual disruptions), resulting in a decline in tourism to the Republic. This, combined with a sluggish local economy, means tax revenues are below expected levels, which means in turn that investment in various infrastructure projects is either delayed or proceeding more slowly than planned. What's more, the government has to subsidize some projects that can't pay for themselves (e.g., public transport fares).

What's specifically new to this scenario are the following points:

- The government has tried to keep inflation to less than 6 percent, but the rising cost of fuel and other imports has made this difficult. Deficits have also started rising, after years of gradually falling.
- New business ventures have been limited.
- The poor local economy is forcing educated citizens to look for jobs overseas. The shortage of technicians means the hoped-for global tech center is having problems.
- A proposal to link the Republic to the nearest continent (and from there the rest of the world) by submarine optical fiber cable has been deferred until the domestic economy recovers.
- Only 60 percent of the country's households have electricity 24 hours a day.

Now What?

One of the immediate benefits of the scenario planning exercise was that it identified the impending collapse in the tourism industry before management or the government was aware it might happen.

In the workshop, Wilson Fyffe, head of the Amplios team, said there was an air of disbelief when the "doom and gloom" scenario was being considered, one of the executives even exclaiming, "This is impossible! If such a downturn occurs, 40% of the businesses in this country will go bankrupt!" One of the other executives made a mobile phone call and could be seen through the glass walls to be pacing up and down the corridor outside the conference room. After 30 minutes on the phone, he came back in and said, "It's true. Travel agents have just told me the South Koreans are now cancelling all their forward travel bookings for next year."

On a more positive note, one of the business opportunities identified in the scenarios came to be active during the following year. This was a joint venture with a European organization for the development of pharmaceuticals based on tropical marine biology.

Wanting to be ready for any of the scenarios to materialize, the Republic's government decided in 2010 to put together a plan to generate some substantial cash reserves that could be used to develop much-needed domestic housing programs.

Amplios came up with a novel idea to raise cash: Why not monetize some of the country's most obvious assets by leasing a few of the islands themselves? However, rather than turning to the hotel industry to develop another resort, Amplios visualized a new market segment that could also be approached: corporate or academic institutions that might consider developing and operating think-tank facilities on the islands. A 55-year lease was priced at $12 million (to be paid upfront).

Four islands in the northern half of the Republic were selected as leasing candidates, and a marketing campaign got under way to find interested parties. Who would like to have their very own R&D/training/conference center-cum-resort on a tropical island paradise?

HOW TO REFORM A SECTOR THAT FEEDS A BILLION PEOPLE

Over the coming years, much of the world's agricultural sector is going to be profoundly affected by a number of global trends happening now. Agriculture—and the entire rural way of life—will acutely feel the impact of such changes as:

- Overall population growth, which will put more stress on the ability of agricultural producers to grow the food required to feed millions of additional hungry mouths

- Increasing urbanization, which not only reduces the amount of arable land as cities spread into the countryside, but lures workers away from agricultural jobs

- The emergence of an enormous new middle class in the developing world that will be enjoying higher incomes and want to eat more, and more varied, food than their parents' generation

- Increasing threats to the natural resource base underpinning agriculture, especially water

- Technological developments that are improving agricultural productivity

Nowhere will changes like these come into sharper focus than in India, a country of over a billion people, where agriculture is still largely oriented toward self-sufficiency rather than fulfilling market needs.

In fact, agriculture in India has become relatively stagnant. Splitting up holdings between one generation and the next has led to farmers' living on the edge of poverty, with the government having to intervene whenever there has been a shock to the system, for example when energy prices have risen. The result is a regulatory patchwork and a complex system of subsidies, both of which contribute to a lack of dynamism in the sector. More than 125 million farm families are locked into a rigid system with the government.

How can Indian agriculture be reformed?

A SCENARIO APPROACH TO THE FUTURE

In 2004, the Indian government teamed up with the World Bank to study this challenge. The idea was to help transform Indian agriculture into a sector with a greater market orientation and the potential to generate income and jobs. To do this job effectively, the government understood that three requirements would have to be met:

1. Across the entire value chain, innovation (technological as well as institutional) was needed.
2. An environment would have to be created in which agricultural holdings could be consolidated to achieve the necessary scale.
3. People displaced by the process would need to have jobs they could fall back on.

What's more, major investments would have to be made in agricultural research and technology, but these investments would pay off only over a relatively long period of time. That's because agriresearch projects tend to stretch over several years, and then the process of implementing the results, especially in a country as large as India, could take several years more.

Yet decisions about how to invest had to be made now.

Thus, right from the outset, leaders in the Indian government recognized they were in a classic scenario planning situation: How could they best make big, expensive decisions about the future, potentially affecting millions of people, if they didn't know how the future would develop?

Two departments within the World Bank that were working with India at the time, South Asia Agriculture and Rural Development (SASAR) and Agriculture and Rural Development (ARD), proposed that a scenario planning process could provide valuable guidance. Such a process would address the key uncertainties and help ensure that India would be well prepared for any future that might emerge, with appropriate agricultural policies and well-placed investments.

They also believed that a key benefit of such a process would be to give the participants, in the words of the organizers, "a chance to develop a shared perspective on a future that is not necessarily a continuation of the past." This was an important consideration in a country where collaboration among different actors (e.g., private and public) did not take place automatically in the agricultural sector, and some practices had barely changed in literally thousands of years!

PULLING A TEAM TOGETHER

SASAR and ARD were to manage the project, and their first decision was to invite the national director of the country's National Agriculture Innovation Project (NAIP) as Indian coleader. To facilitate the scenario planning process, the World Bank chose Kees van der Heijden, formerly in charge of Strategic Planning at Shell and one of scenario planning's true heavy hitters, and his colleague Ron Bradfield. The process kicked off at World Bank Headquarters in Washington and moved from there to Mumbai.

Here, it was clear that experts in politics, economics, ecology, and Indian society and culture were needed as part of the group. Further, if the project was going to be successful, high-level participation was required. The final roster of the group comprised a who's who from this sector:

- Farm leaders
- Senior officials from the Ministry of Agriculture
- The director general (DG) and several deputy DGs of the Indian Council of Agricultural Research (ICAR)
- Vice-chancellors of several state agriculture universities
- Senior executives from seed and agrochemical industries and agricultural credit organizations
- Leaders of agricultural processing, trade, and marketing organizations
- Senior NGO leaders

- Donor representatives
- Experts on agricultural development

SETTING THE GOALS OF THE GAME

What could this exercise realistically hope to achieve? Like all good scenario planners, van der Heijden and Bradfield made sure to state clearly for the participants that it was not an attempt to predict the future. Instead, its objective was to provide insights to the Indian government that would make it easier to make the necessary decisions that would address these two questions:

First, how can India's agricultural systems be positioned so that they can be successful under different conditions?

The idea here was that Indian agriculture must be able to respond to whatever big changes may occur over the next 10 to 15 years. Accordingly, decision makers would not only need to formulate wise policies but also design the actual institutions that would carry them out.

Second, what technologies should India be pursuing, and what role should the Indian agricultural research system play?

In addition, the group also decided that it would be essential for the exercise to always keep in mind the three fundamental goals that would underlie any future strategy, namely, the need to:

- Feed the people
- Sustain resources
- Promote trade

GETTING STARTED

The first step in the scenario process was to gain some background understanding of the issues and trends affecting agriculture in India. A number of so-called remarkable people were selected to be interviewed— experts from different stakeholder groups such as government, farmers, the private sector, academic institutions, and international aid agencies.

Their input would help the scenario team develop a clearer view of the uncertainties facing the agricultural sector over the long run.

"Remarkable People" Are Asked a Tough Question

Eleven "remarkable" experts were selected for personal interviews conducted in New Delhi. The were asked one basic question:

"When thinking of the future of Indian agriculture,
what keeps you awake at night?"

This simple formulation was an excellent way to elicit the issues and concerns that reflected the key uncertainties the sector would face over the next few years.

The experts' answers were clustered into four main themes:

1. *Water*. Will there be enough for future generations? How can India ensure its sustainability?

2. *Government or market*. Which will play the dominant role in driving Indian agricultural progress in the future?

3. *Rural communities*. How will they change as agricultural practices evolve, and how fast will the ongoing shift of population from rural areas to cities take place?

4. *Rural stakeholders*. How will they be able to make their voices heard?

These themes were then presented to the main group of participants in the scenario process, who confirmed that they were of critical importance.

DRIVING FORCES

The main scenario group then convened in a workshop in Mumbai. About two dozen people participated. Building on the input from the "remarkable people" consulted, this group's first task was to develop a view of the main forces they believed would be driving Indian agricultural development between 2005 and 2030—a 25-year time horizon.

In all, the group came up with some 200 individual suggestions for driving forces. As is customary in scenario workshops, these 200 drivers were written by the participants on Post-it notes and stuck up on the walls around the workshop room.

The next step was to group them into broad categories. In this case, the drivers all fell into one of nine themes, deemed to be the nine big areas of change that would likely have a significant impact on how Indian agriculture develops through 2030. These nine themes were:

1. Governance and policies
2. The legal environment
3. Social issues
4. The macroeconomic environment
5. Markets
6. Knowledge and information
7. Farmers
8. Natural resources
9. Climate change

Similarly detailed items formed the content of the other categories. The 200 ideas to consider thus ranged very widely, from the availability of credit and changing family structures to shifting land use, the conservatism of farmers, and the effect of biotech on productivity.

Nine themes were nonetheless too many to work with. To simplify further, the cause-and-effect relationships between these nine themes were discussed, and the group was able to distill the very essence of the future uncertainties into just a couple of so-called major dimensions—broad trends that, as the future unfolds, will tend to develop an "either/or" resolution, as we've seen in Chapter 2 of this book.

The major dimensions were defined as the following:

- *Economic management*. Would India's economy tend to become more liberalized and market-based. . . or more state-controlled and centrally managed?

- *Social fabric*. Would rural people be able to look after themselves adequately, living well-organized lives within their villages. . . or would social cohesion be weak, resulting in India's poor people being marginalized even further?

- *Global warming*. Would it hit India hard, creating agricultural production and water management difficulties. . . or would India be spared?

30 PROPOSALS

The team did their work well! They came up with 200 ideas, which were then grouped into nine overarching categories.

To illustrate the depth of their thinking, here are 30 driving forces that members of the scenario group came up with, which then became the category "Markets":

COMMERCIALIZATION OF AGRICULTURE

LACK OF MARKETS

EXCHANGE OPPORTUNITIES, MULTIFUNCTIONAL

URBANIZATION

GLOBAL TRADING OPPORTUNITIES

MARKET STRUCTURE DEVELOPMENT

QUALITY STANDARDS

CREATION OF BRANDS TO INCREASE VALUE-ADDED FOR FARMERS

PREFERENCES OF CONSUMERS

GLOBAL COMPETITION AND COLLABORATION

DOMESTIC MARKET REFORMS

INFRASTRUCTURE DEVELOPMENT

STRENGTHEN LOCAL MARKET, SWADESI [PATRIOTIC SELF-SUFFICIENCY]

SHIFTING DIETARY PATTERNS

CHANGING DEMAND
FOR FOOD

POTENTIAL HIGH-VALUE
LIVESTOCK PRODUCTS

PRIVATE SECTOR
DEVELOPMENT

PRIVATE SECTOR
PARTNERSHIPS

COST OF ENERGY

PRICE OF ENERGY

CAPITAL MARKETS

MARKET CREDIT

RISK MANAGEMENT

RISK MANAGEMENT
AND INSURANCE

ROLE OF MULTINATIONAL
COMPANIES

SUPERMARKETS

"SUPERMARKETIZATION"

LONG-TERM VALUES VERSUS
"SUPERMARKETISM"

COST EFFICIENCY

CONTRACT FARMING

The Scenario Matrix: First Attempt

The group now proceeded to posit Indian development scenarios based on the combination of these major dimensions. However, in order to create a conventional 2 × 2 matrix defining the scenarios, they opted to focus on only the first two dimensions for the time being.

Thus, with 200 drivers and nine themes to think about, the key either/or developments boiled down to these:

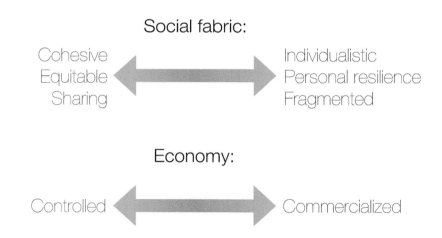

Social fabric:

Cohesive
Equitable
Sharing

Individualistic
Personal resilience
Fragmented

Economy:

Controlled

Commercialized

As for the third major dimension, global warming, instead of considering it as an either/or factor in each one of the four resulting scenarios, they decided that a rapidly warming world would be built into one of the scenarios. So the scenario matrix looked like this:

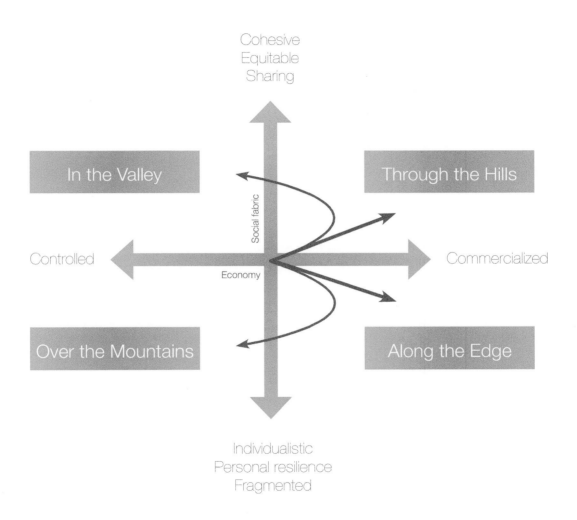

Cohesive
Equitable
Sharing

In the Valley

Through the Hills

Social fabric

Controlled

Economy

Commercialized

Over the Mountains

Along the Edge

Individualistic
Personal resilience
Fragmented

Historically, India's economy had been controlled but heading down a liberalization path. So the implied starting point for all four scenarios was that market liberalization would continue. However, in two of the four scenarios, this trend would be reversed (see black arrows).

The group named the four scenarios "In the Valley," "Through the Hills," "Along the Edge," and "Over the Mountains."

SCENARIO: "CONTROLLED ECONOMY + COHESIVE SOCIETY"

The starting point for the scenario called **"In the Valley"** was the idea that India's desire for social cohesion meant that the country would be willing to accept a significant degree of government control of the economy. Hence, the arrow you see in the preceding graphic changes directions and heads backward.

There's a price to pay for this social equity, however, and that is relatively low economic growth (3 percent) and only slow improvements in productivity. On the upside, although economic growth is modest, most members of society participate and benefit.

This is the scenario in which the group posited severe global warming effects.

SCENARIO: "COMMERCIALIZED ECONOMY + COHESIVE SOCIETY"

In **"Through the Hills,"** the country's concerns for cohesion are also strong, but equally important, India wants to allow market incentives to spur productivity gains. Sometimes, however, these two goals clash. This is especially the case when the system has to absorb some kind of external shock, or when choices have to be made that don't allow for easy compromises between these goals.

The group posited that in these instances, social goals would take priority over economic ones. Even so, over the 30 years to come, India would create a sound basis for a market economy.

SCENARIO: "COMMERCIALIZED ECONOMY + FRAGMENTED SOCIETY"

"Along the Edge" is the scenario where India's top priority is economic development. To accomplish this, the country is prepared to allow greater social inequalities, under the assumption that these disparities would act as an incentive driving greater productivity.

In the words of the World Bank report, "This scenario explores how far such a view could be taken before inequity becomes so intolerable that the 'collective' must step in to moderate the worst manifestations of market power." In other words, this scenario tiptoes around the idea that in its own interest, society will at some point limit development and growth.

SCENARIO: "CONTROLLED ECONOMY + COMMERCIALIZED SOCIETY"

In the future dubbed **"Over the Mountains,"** market liberalization has proceeded so far that it has led to a free-for-all society—so much so that people actually demand a return to a more controlled economy.

In this scenario, the group explores the effects of strong but positive government controls. They posit a number of difficulties arising, but ultimately foresee a positive resolution.

The Scenario Matrix: Second Attempt

Draft narratives describing these four scenarios were then written up in detail and reviewed by the members of the group. Rather than keeping the drafts in-house, it was decided to show them to a number of outside experts and get their validation and feedback. These outsiders to the process spotted some inconsistencies and made several suggestions for revisions.

For example, "Over the Mountains" was seen as problematical by many of the experts. They insisted that in India's democratic system, it would not be possible for the government to step in and interfere with the agricultural sector in the way the scenario was written—unless there were some kind of emergency.

Thus, an emergency was written into the scenario. This addition to the story improved its overall coherence, said the scenario writers. It generated a greater feeling of plausibility.

The experts also had a whole raft of suggestions for details that were not included in the scenarios and for changes that would improve their internal consistency. These ranged from technical issues (e.g., water management and security considerations) to policy matters (e.g., whether and how foreign direct investment in agriculture might take place).

The scenario team went back to the drawing board. This time, they emerged with clearer and crisper scenario narratives. The four scenarios still had the same names as before, but their parameters were defined in a clearer way; they told slightly different stories.

The revised scenarios are shown in the graphic to the right. This time around, the language used to define the major dimensions (which would become the axes of the scenario matrix) was massaged. Remember, these axes define the key uncertainties for the future, either one alternative or the other.

These dimensions were now described like this:

- What will India's society consider to be its key values in the future—equity and equality, or productivity and efficiency?
- In terms of the Indian economy, and the choice that citizens have over how it is organized and managed, will there be a tendency toward government intervention, or greater liberalization?

The new 2030 scenarios were fleshed out in detail, as demonstrated in the descriptions on the following pages.

Feedback from outside experts is very valuable!

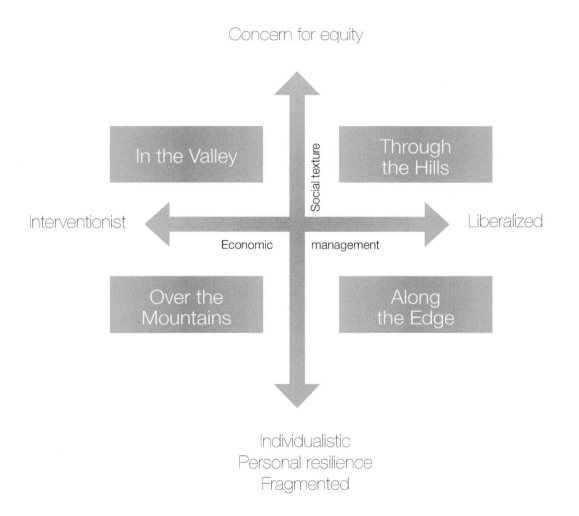

Concern for equity

Social texture

In the Valley

Through
the Hills

Interventionist   Liberalized

Economic   management

Over the
Mountains

Along
the Edge

Individualistic
Personal resilience
Fragmented

REVISED SCENARIO: "IN THE VALLEY".

Agricultural policies have focused on increasing the amount of irrigated land and introducing new technologies rather than on improving the scale of farming operations. However, despite advances made, this approach means that subsistence farming continues, and farm incomes remain low. Meanwhile, the manufacturing sector is not growing fast enough, so it cannot absorb displaced farm workers, resulting in migration back to the villages. Agricultural reform and consolidation into larger, more efficient operations have failed.

India's service economy is booming, however. Unfortunately, its growth brings about an increasing gap between the country's rich and poor, and this disparity is fueling resentments, calling India's social and cultural values into question. Eventually this increasingly intolerable situation generates enough political pressure that in elections about halfway into the scenario period, the country swings to the left, with the electorate calling for a more interventionist approach toward planning the economy.

Highly progressive taxes and income redistribution then become the key tools allowing the government to establish the social safety net that protects the poorest and most vulnerable members of society from the mercilessness of the business cycle.

Speaking of protection, by 2030, new regulations and protectionist trade measures have made India a less attractive country to invest in. As a consequence, economic growth stagnates, and the country pulls away from the global economy, even dropping out of the WTO.

Here is a 2030 vignette from this scenario, excerpted from the World Bank report:

> The rain-fed sorghum farmer is living a relatively safe life: there is an assured public sector agricultural produce market for the little that s/he can produce. Basanti, a village woman, finds

herself facing a less competitive, low-equilibrium world in which a few new varieties of rice/wheat are provided from the public research system. As a small farmer in this system, she has no choices to make because the State and the local agricultural production committees decide on land and water use. The need for rain-fed sorghum is reinforced by the worsening water scarcity. The poultry industry is no longer the major consumer of rain-fed sorghum. Even this low-quality sorghum is essential now—but labeled as nutritious food—to maintain food security. The little that is produced is processed by local women's self-help groups and supplied to local schools for their mid-day meals and to local hospitals. Despite a wave of neo-nationalism and socially responsible women leaders at the helm reinventing traditional food, there is little growth in the processing/livestock industry. Without enough growth and external support to fuel investment, any additional supply of meat/processed food—even equipment for food processing—comes from China.

The government-led interventionist approach to the economy means that when farmers face an unexpected problem or challenge, they expect that the government will step in and help them. Politicians know how important the rural vote is, so they ensure that this approach continues. The rural electorate looks to government for decisions concerning resource allocation, too. At one point in the scenario period, water becomes scarce, and the state has to devise a rationing plan.

REVISED SCENARIO: "ALONG THE EDGE"

In many ways, this scenario is the opposite of the previous one. In "Along the Edge," Indian society has come to accept that prosperity will come to only those who are productively employed. For the poor, equality of opportunity is considered more valuable than the empty rhetoric of social equality.

In 2030, the government's priority is to make the country more competitive. This has meant improving education as well as access to finance, since both are considered to be elements that will fuel economic growth.

But in making these gains, certain social trade-offs have had to be accepted. For example, more and more marginalized people have become squatters on the edges of the big cities, and the government has not only allowed this to continue, but even institutionalized the squatters' rights. Crime is on the rise, and with it a feeling of insecurity.

The main challenge for the government is to strike the balance between creating incentives to boost productivity and growth, and controlling the social unrest that this brings about. To create a healthy liberalized market, the government relaxed regulations and restrictions. Investment poured in, and development was rapid. Bureaucracy, infrastructure, reliability of distribution—all these saw great improvements.

What about agriculture? Consolidation moved forward quickly, and in the newly competitive world, the small subsistence farmer "became extinct," as the report put it. These farmers migrated to the cities where they had little difficulty finding jobs in the manufacturing sector, although it was difficult for them to leave the land that had been in their families for generations. Farm laborers had a tougher time finding jobs; unemployment among this group is still high.

Meanwhile, this land was snapped up by large mechanized agricultural enterprises that invested heavily in equipment and other technologies,

and there was an additional knock-on effect of this investment: It spurred productivity growth not only in the agricultural sector itself, but also in the technology companies supplying it. Now these large farms were promoting local development of downstream activities—more growth in rural areas.

Here is the World Bank's 2030 vignette:

> Three friends from the last batch educated in entirely public sector universities meet for a reunion. They find their lives reshaped, and their fortunes and commitments taking different turns. Massive out-migration from agriculture (especially of small farmers and landless labor forced by the market to seek some livelihood in urban areas or in the villages) has forced Arpita to take up the cause of health and well being of the people who are now living on the edge of crisis and are increasingly prone to social tensions/crime. She makes vain attempts to get the State and other private players interested in health and healthy sorghum-based diets. However, sorghum and other feed grain are now grown for the growing livestock/meat processing industry and export. Industrial investment in villages provides some employment—especially to skilled labor. Sandeep's growing agribusiness takes over Pizza Hut, and builds other vertical linkages (wheat and other grain mills, investing in massive corporate farms, poultry and dairy industries). Major investments by poultry industry, farms, manufacturers and service providers (cold storage, packing, transport) and increasing profits for these investments are ensured by Ramesh, the third of this batch of friends who turned to politics.

Rain-fed sorghum production is limited to some large farms in the absolutely dry parts of the country; the other farms produce feed grain/

fodder, buying their water requirements. The large number of unemployed are given food cards—a drain on the economy no doubt, but a necessary evil supported by food imports from other grain-producing countries. Economic growth can afford this drain!

In short, the Indian economy has done very well, but in terms of income disparities and social cohesion, there's been a high price to pay. By 2030, however, rural poverty is being tackled.

REVISED SCENARIO: "OVER THE MOUNTAINS"

This future has India mandating the consolidation of the country's agricultural system as a top-down project. This has been deemed necessary, thanks to a crisis; although the scenario doesn't specify what has happened, exactly, we can gather it is some combination of natural disaster and water shortage. Global warming is also an issue that has also been having a serious impact on agriculture. The country's important cereal crops may not meet the hoped-for improvements in yield, leading to food security issues.

As if these problems weren't difficult enough, energy prices have skyrocketed and the US dollar has tumbled, causing a global recession. Relations with China are tense. Large-scale terrorism is still a threat. "Generally, people felt insecure," says the report.

That's possibly an understatement, because—wait—there's more. Avian flu, spread by air travelers, has killed millions worldwide. The result has been a calamitous drop in travel and trade worldwide, making the recession even worse.

Against this horrific backdrop, the Indian people have demanded that the government do something, and the the first sector to insist on action was agriculture. In response, the government set out to reorganize the sector region by region, combining small farms into large, more viable ones.

The move was mandatory. To alleviate the unemployment that this would cause to those small farmers and laborers who lost their work, public-private

partnerships were formed to offer alternative employment. These initiatives solved one problem, but they have created another: By taking up the slack in the more remote and economically unattractive areas of the country where no private investment was forthcoming, the government has become an economic layer that is depended upon as a crutch, requiring more and more regulation.

Here is a vignette from 2030 in this scenario:

> Sukhram used to be a "model farmer." He himself now finds that difficult to believe. He had a marginal farm on which he grew wheat, grain, and fodder; and had a dairy with four buffaloes and a few birds, too. He feels that the economy is growing well. However, his farm is now part of a large District Coop Farm, under the Haryana State Government. He no longer thinks of cultivating sorghum or even wheat––and has no incentive to tell these urban-bred farm managers and scientists about some of his local crop management techniques: "Why should we produce more? I can live off the food plus meat cards given to us under the Social Security Scheme—it's PDS for the Underprivileged." The last straw was when Bakshi Seeds (a well-meaning and highly informed seed producer and trader) went out of business, and Bakshi migrated to Australia to be with his son. After that, there was no one left in the village to discuss market trends or feed mixtures for poultry that the industry was trying out.

> Sukhram believes that the multinational companies cheated poor farmers and exploited labor. Getting information from the Seeds Division of HAU (which took over Bakshi's firm) is next to impossible, with forms to fill and hours to wait—"and our consolidated farm does not need all that anyway with the State Civil Supplies Corp. buying up all our produce." Rain-fed sorghum is not a popular crop, but in dry areas in which nothing else grows,

> there is still a demand; and the State poultry/dairy units do use it for feed grain. Sukhram's son-in-law knows about the minor millets grown for these purposes and for food supply in the burgeoning slums. "With no new investment coming in, and cutthroat competition for jobs, these slum dwellers are lucky they have a State that gives them at least a sorghum meal."

The report concludes that the reformed and reorganized agricultural sector is able to stand on its own two feet, and subsidies are being phased out. But the overall situation is increasingly difficult to manage.

REVISED SCENARIO: "THROUGH THE HILLS"

There is an all-pervasive mood of optimism in this scenario, a will to undertake what is right for the economy. This positive attitude provides leeway to the government to advance reforms, and it is also the basis for private investment in rural India, which had been neglected for so long.

"A shared belief that productivity must contribute to social progress and vice versa" has led to the view that rural India is no longer seen as a problem area but a potential market with big economic potential in its own right.

Everything started with the understanding that economies of scale would be the key to the success of the country's attempt to reform its agricultural sector. Consolidation was a must. But rather than allowing displaced farmers to suffer, the country's manufacturing sector would also have to grow, in order to absorb and redeploy the farm workers who would be out of work when the country's small farms were reorganized.

The government therefore put coherent policies in place to first increase investments in rural areas and assist them to develop; this would later allow people to move off the land not as destitute peasants but with some savings. For this to work, an attractive investment climate was needed. The government put reforms in place, but gradually, and helped affected sectors and people during the transition period.

Education, training, and infrastructure also received attention. Government bureaucracy was streamlined and made more transparent in many business-friendly ways, and labor laws were also modernized. With all these improvements, investment began to flow into the country. This was particularly the case in light manufacturing (e.g., shoes and textiles), where India's skilled workforce and cost advantages made a difference.

The following is a 2030 vignette from "Through the Hills":

A steady phase of development, led by a strong sense of social cohesion and responsibility in an upbeat, entrepreneurial atmosphere presents a pleasant transformation of the rural economy in Bihar to Ajit, an NRI who comes visiting after 25 years' absence. Ajit left India in the midst of a crisis in which increasing privatization and an indifferent State had made life difficult. He comes back to find his village transformed to a neat, peaceful locality with healthy, educated residents. Ajit's brothers (Ramu, a political leader, and Kesav, a poultry exporter) and his sister (Anita, a teacher with various social and civic engagements) are leading highly fulfilling lives. An uncle heads the transport service agency.

This transformation in rural Bihar, they tell him, came with the conscious choice of trade-led growth with a socially enforced norm (enforced through active policy advocacy) to promote rural employment. As capital was drawn in by the new investment-friendly climate, and with productive local economic involvement in every enterprise or industry promoted, private sector investment in research, health, infrastructure, and education also grew. This investment was largely private, within civic regulations/norms. As employment in the rural nonfarm sector grew and people moved out of agriculture, farm sizes increased, providing options for the focused use of land and crops, such as rain-fed sorghum for the poultry industry. The diverse range of consumers for Bihar's poultry products (a variety of new meats, too, under major global food brands and local ones) led to better and more profitable enterprises in and around the livestock sector, and more local employment, better incomes, living conditions, and lifestyles.

The incentive of being able to find an attractive alternative job in one of India's burgeoning manufacturing outfits proved to be the key to enticing small farmers to leave the land and consolidate their holdings in large, professionally managed agribusinesses. One hundred million farmers and farm workers were successfully resettled. The entire program was seen as "a prime example of how the combination of economic reality with Indian values could achieve superior results."

Epilogue

The participants in this wide-ranging scenario planning exercise chose a very long time horizon for their glimpse into the future—25 years. It's natural, then, that after just five or six years, none of the four scenarios seems to be dominating, although certain trends are becoming clear for the moment, such as higher energy prices.

"What we've also seen," said Riikka Rajalahti of the World Bank, the project's director, "is the development of a very wealthy group of urbanites, well linked in and trusting the market economy, with large groups of other people who remain more on the outside of the developments. Protest movements of groups that are not happy have emerged, like around the Nano plant in West Bengal."

Discussions of free trade in agriculture began to take place after the first food crisis in 2008–2009. All of these elements were included in the scenarios, "even though they may be playing out in other ways than we expected in 2006," Riikka said.

What happened next? "The scenario process overall—its ability to open our minds and catalyze collaboration among different actors—was highly influential on the National Agriculture Innovation Project. The government has been very happy with this game-changing project. In fact, they are so happy that they are now considering a new phase with even greater attention to entrepreneurial understanding among researchers and their programs."

Case Study: VisitScotland

SCOTLAND WANTS YOU TO VISIT

Vacation coming up? Spend a few days in Scotland—and please drop a few quid into the local economy while you're at it.

How should Scotland entice you to do this? What investments does the country need to make today to improve its chances that tomorrow, of all the places you might choose as your vacation destination, you will pick Scotland?

That is the essence of tourism development. And the answer to this important question is: It depends. It depends on how, over the next few years, a number of factors and trends develop that have the potential to help, or harm, the future of Scottish tourism.

In 2002, executives of VisitScotland, the country's tourism authority, understood that before they could recommend policies, plans, and investments that would promote the growth of tourism in Scotland, it would be a good idea to gain some insight into how the future might unfold.

FIRST, SOME PERSPECTIVE

Some 200 countries worldwide currently invest significant amounts of money, time, and personnel on efforts and programs to develop their tourism industries. In addition, countless cities, states, and regions do, too—usually, but not always, with smaller budgets. The city of San Francisco alone had a 2010–2011 budget of $24 million to spend on tourism development.

It's easy to see why this makes sense. Tourism is huge business—the number one industry in the world. In 2010, the United Nations World Tourism Organization (UNWTO) clocked 940 million international tourist arrivals, an increase of almost 7 percent from the previous year—not bad in the middle of a gloomy economic downturn. Taking all those international

trips together, travelers spent a whopping $919 billion in the countries they visited that year.

What country (or, for that matter, what one-horse town) wouldn't want to get its hands on as much of that money as possible? Just about everyone would like a piece of this delicious, and continuously growing, tourism pie. That is why, sooner or later, many governments find themselves in the tourism development business.

Even though it's a huge industry, tourism is very competitive. A couple in Manchester with a week's vacation coming up and just a few hundred pounds to spend has a huge array of destinations they could afford. For the same price as a holiday in London or Edinburgh, they could easily find plane-plus-hotel packages that would allow them to spend that week on the beach on Corfu or playing golf in Portugal. It is no exaggeration to say that a ski resort in the Swiss Alps is in competition not just with the resort on the next mountain over, or even with a ski resort in the Austrian Alps, but with a beach destination in Thailand and a theme park in Orlando. That is how broad the options are for tourists—and why being competitive is so important.

In 2010, the country that took the largest share of tourism's $919 billion dollars was the United States ($103 billion, about 11 percent of the total). France, though, perennially tops the chart in terms of international arrivals. In 2010, for example, France logged 28 percent more arrivals from outside the country than did the United States, which was ranked a fairly distant number two (77 million versus 60 million). Following the United States, China (56 million), Spain (53 million), and Italy (44 million) round out the world's top five destinations.

Rank	Country	International Tourist Arrivals	Change 2010/2009
1	France	76.8 million	+0.0%
2	United States	59.7 million	+8.7%
3	China	55.7 million	+9.4%
4	Spain	52.7 million	+1.0%
5	Italy	43.6 million	+0.9%
6	United Kingdom	28.1 million	−0.2%
7	Turkey	27.0 million	+5.9%
8	Germany	26.9 million	+10.9%
9	Malaysia	24.6 million	+3.9%
10	Mexico	22.4 million	+4.4%

WHAT ABOUT SCOTLAND?

With 28 million arrivals, the United Kingdom was ranked number six in the world in 2010, and placed number seven in terms of tourism receipts ($30.4 billion). As part of the United Kingdom, Scotland's arrivals and receipts are buried in the UNWTO's figures for the United Kingdom as a whole, but we can turn to the statistics generated by Scotland's tourism development authority, VisitScotland, for some detail. According to these data, tourists from overseas pumped about £1.44 billion (approximately $2.3 billion) into the Scottish economy in 2010, or about 8 percent of the UK total. Going back to the UNWTO's figures for each country's income generated by tourism, Scotland therefore ranks a bit behind Finland and Slovenia and a bit ahead of Cyprus and Slovakia when it comes to generating tourist dollars from foreigners. Outside Europe, the countries that are in the same ballpark as Scotland are Peru, Tunisia, and the Philippines.

Rank	Country	International Tourist Receipts (2010)
1	United States	$103.5 billion
2	Spain	$52.5 billion
3	France	$46.3 billion
4	China	$45.8 billion
5	Italy	$38.8 billion
6	Germany	$34.7 billion
7	United Kingdom	$30.4 billion
8	Australia	$30.1 billion
9	Hong Kong (China)	$23.0 billion
10	Turkey	$20.8 billion

However, Scotland enjoys a large source of tourism revenues that don't show up in these international statistics: England. Visitors to Scotland from other parts of Britain account for about twice as much spending in the country as international travelers do. Including these intra-UK visitors, the total volume of Scotland's tourism receipts is three times the overseas figure, or about £4.1 billion ($6.5 billion).

SCENARIO PLANNING TO THE RESCUE

Now let's cast our minds back to the early 2000s. That is when the VisitScotland executives began thinking about the challenge: How could Scotland successfully increase its share of international as well as British tourism? Before generating concrete plans, however, they thought it would be prudent as well as instructive to formulate a vision of how the future landscape for Scottish tourism might change over the next few years. They wanted to get an idea of the different directions in which the future might unfold so that they could develop tourism strategies that would be not only effective but flexible as well.

With the appointment of Philip Riddle as CEO in 2002 (whose background had been at Shell Oil, an outspoken champion of scenario planning), it was decided that this technique would be of value to the organization, particularly since, just then, Britain was facing some major uncertainties, such as how a local outbreak of foot-and-mouth disease might affect tourism, and what the impact could be of the looming war in Iraq.

To explore these possibilities in detail, and to help guide a strategic conversation about the future, VisitScotland brought in an outside consultant, Ian Yeoman, who was not only one of the world's foremost thinkers on the future of tourism, but also a strong believer in scenario planning.

In 2003, a high-powered team was assembled to work together creating future scenarios. It consisted of representatives from several organizations considered stakeholders in the future of Scotland's tourism: VisitScotland,

Historic Scotland, Caledonian McBrayn, Scottish National Heritage, the Forestry Commission, the Scottish Arts Council, Highlands and Islands Enterprise, Scottish Enterprise, and, of course, the Scottish government itself.

This team got to work analyzing the key drivers of Scotland's tourism industry, the first step in the process of creating plausible tourism scenarios for Scotland in the year 2015.

After discussion and analysis, these drivers were identified:

EXCHANGE RATES

GDP

GOVERNANCE

HEALTH

FISCAL POLICY

SAFETY

DISPOSABLE INCOME

PRICE SENSITIVITY/
YIELD

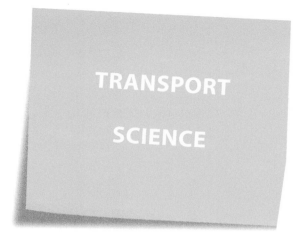

TRANSPORT

SCIENCE

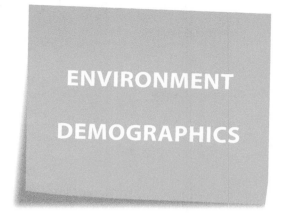

ENVIRONMENT

DEMOGRAPHICS

PERCEPTUAL
VALUES

MEDIA

HISTORY

LEISURE ACTIVITIES

After examining how these drivers would interact with each other, the scenario team grouped them into major dimensions of the future (i.e., the axes that would graphically represent the two broadest and most important uncertainties regarding the future).

"Tourism has flourished in Scotland since Victorian times and has the potential to be the key pillar, if not the bedrock, of the economy 100 years from now. One thing is certain: tourism will be here in 2015. It is an industry which cannot be outsourced to India or Hungary, as are financial services and call centers. It is an industry which will last longer than oil and gas, when these resources are exhausted. More importantly, it is an industry which represents the nation's identity, values and culture. Tourism is synonymous with Scotland—they are inseparable."

Excerpt from Ian Yeoman's Report for VisitScotland

In terms of Scotland's future economic environment, the alternative outcomes (not necessarily opposites of each other) were identified as:

Deflation
Disinflation ⟷ Prosperity

The other major dimension was considered to be "consumer propensity" (i.e., the way consumers would tend to behave in 2015). Its outcomes were deemed to be:

Price
sensitivity ⟷ Sophistication

Combining these two dimensions into the old familiar 2 × 2 matrix, the following scenarios emerged, which were named by the scenario team as shown:

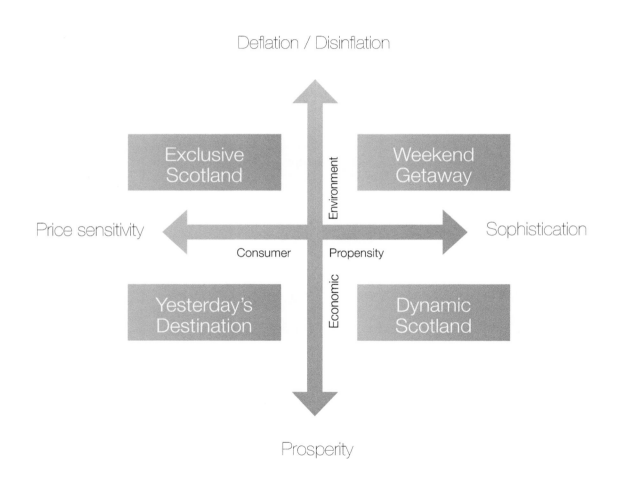

Four contrasting scenarios were thus defined based on the combination of economic factors (prosperity or deflation) and consumer attitude toward spending (price sensitivity or sophistication).

The scenarios were as follows:

- **"Dynamic Scotland,"** in which tourism would become the number one industry in Scotland, generating £10 billion in annual receipts—more than double the 2004 status quo.

- **"Weekend Getaway,"** in which tourism would be based more on consumerism and play.

- **"Yesterday's Destination,"** a scenario where tourism would primarily be backward-looking, where the industry would remain complacent, uncompetitive, and slow-growing.

- **"Exclusive Scotland,"** though the name certainly sounds good, was the scenario resulting from the *failure* of the Scottish economy. Deflation would be harming the local economy, but with exchange rates favoring international visitors, high-spending tourists would flock to Scotland's high-priced and exclusive resorts.

Next, Yeoman and his crew fleshed out these four scenarios, describing each one from the perspective of 2015. Let's take a look.

SCENARIO: "DYNAMIC SCOTLAND"

In 2015, tourism has become Scotland's number one industry. It employs 350,000 people, generates more revenue than any other part of the Scottish economy, and has gained in prestige and recognition.

The economic prosperity enjoyed in this scenario has come about thanks to a number of factors, among them the favorable exchange rate of the pound, high disposable incomes, low income taxes, reduced gasoline taxes, and infrastructure investments.

Scotland is a leading international tourist destination, and it is this international, rather than merely British, attractiveness that is the key to this scenario. "A realization came across the world that everything Scottish and Celtic had cultural capital and acclaim"—from Sir Walter Scott to comedian Billy Connolly.

In the decade leading to 2015, the country launched several successful programs. For example, "110 Percent Scotland" focuses on culture and heritage. "HQ Scotland" has fueled massive growth in business tourism. Touring holidays have been positioned to attract upscale travelers with lots of disposable income. A clublike quality assurance program established by VisitScotland has proven to be very successful, helping service providers position themselves within Scotland's tourism portfolio, which consists of a variety of products:

- Playful Scotland
- Contemporary Scotland
- Body, mind, and spirit
- Business tourism
- City breaks
- Touring and exploration

What's more, VisitScotland itself has become a public-private partnership and is well on the way to transforming itself into a wholly private enterprise, as the government sees tourism as healthy and successful enough that it is no longer in need of state intervention. VisitScotland is considered among the best tourism agencies in the world, frequently benchmarked by other countries.

SCENARIO: "WEEKEND GETAWAY"

This scenario revolves around consumers with plenty of disposable income and the increasing competition for their valuable time. Thanks to an economy featuring falling airfares and affordable hotel prices, a weekend jaunt to Scotland should no longer be seen as a full-blown journey but rather as an impulse purchase, a leisure product bought on short notice.

To make this work, Scotland has transformed itself into a destination that is sometimes described as hedonistic, a place where middle-class people can go to indulge themselves in a little affordable luxury.

As emotionally appealing as Scotland's leisure offer may be, if this scenario is to prove successful for VisitScotland, the country still has to stand out among many other options vying for the traveler's time and money.

This is because Scotland is faced with competition in this scenario not so much from other attractive cities in the United Kingdom or Europe, but from completely unrelated alternatives that travelers might opt to spend their money on instead (e.g., on some form of entertainment or even a purchase for their home). Moreover, since this is a deflationary scenario, the price of many of these alternative purchases will be falling, so a new TV is becoming more and more attractive compared to a romantic Caledonian miniholiday.

One of the keys to the success of this scenario is how easy and inexpensive it is to get to Scotland in the first place. Budget airlines and improved rail service have made this a reality. For example, visitors from London and southeast England can now leave their desks at 5:00 p.m. on a Friday evening and be in their Scottish destination city by eight o'clock.

For obvious reasons, this scenario focuses on visitors from Europe rather than the United States and other overseas countries. European visitors identify with Scotland's spirit, culture, and character. One segment of the tourism industry that took off was conferences. Although businesses didn't take advantage of Scotland's conferencing infrastructure (owing to cost-cutting measures and the coming-of-age of videoconferencing), associations and conventions saw Scotland as a great destination for their events.

The country also launched a mandatory certification program to ensure quality in all the various facets of the tourism economy. Competitive businesses made it; others were allowed to go under.

SCENARIO: "YESTERDAY'S DESTINATION"

In a world where exchange rates don't work in Scotland's favor, the short-break market has not taken off—instead, it's the Scots who scurry off on cheap flights for a weekend in Prague or Budapest rather than the other way around. Hoteliers, restaurateurs, and other service providers in Scotland have grown complacent, and the Scottish tourism experience is mainly centered on playing up nostalgia for the country's legendary past—an amalgam of bagpipes, tartans, and haggis.

Compared to "Dynamic Scotland," this scenario foresees the Scottish tourism sector generating only half as much in revenues, employing only half as many people, and growing at a paltry 1 percent per year (compared to Dynamic's *very* dynamic 7 percent). It still represents 4 percent of the country's GDP, so it is not insignificant, but it's in steady decline—a dog in every way.

Why? As a destination, Scotland simply hasn't stayed competitive. The outbound tourist market has grown, and Scotland's product offer couldn't effectively hold its own against these other destinations. Its visitors in 2015 are predominantly British and mostly representative of two segments: "gray and mature" or "with young families" (it's still a safe destination, after all). Health tourism has seen some success, but not enough to make up for the decline in other segments.

In this scenario, the disadvantageous exchange rate has made a Scottish vacation too expensive for what it is. Price-sensitive, value-conscious consumers are staying away in droves.

What's more, the country's certification program, which had the best of intentions, merely *added* to the cost of doing business in the tourism sector, stifling innovation and, in the eyes of hoteliers and restaurateurs, turning VisitScotland into the unpleasant role of enforcers.

> " In mid-summer the high streets of Pitlochry and St. Andrews are still crowded with tourists—but those tourists are spending less, every year there are fewer of them, and for how much longer will they keep returning? "

Excerpt from the Report

SCENARIO: "EXCLUSIVE SCOTLAND"

In 2015, Scotland's economy is in shambles. High unemployment, high costs, price-sensitive consumers lacking disposable income—these factors have led to a collapse of domestic UK tourism.

But that doesn't mean tourism has disappeared entirely from Scotland. The exchange rate is favorable, so wealthy international visitors still come to Scotland to vacation at the country's exclusive luxury resorts. Overall, however, the industry is in free fall, with revenues declining 4 percent a year.

Tourism has dropped from the country's consciousness. It obviously still occupies some local importance here and there, but for the country as a whole, it's dropped off the map.

What about these resorts that are doing so well? For the most part, they're all-inclusive, gated resorts that are owned by foreign rather than Scottish companies. Typically, their guests fly in to enjoy such activities as spas, casinos, or deer stalking, and after a few days they fly out again, never having explored any other parts of the country. With practically all their time spent safe and secure in their resort compound, these international visitors rarely have any contact with the local population.

Meanwhile, for the British market, Scotland has devolved into a second-class destination, revolving around visiting friends and relatives and "cheap-and-cheerful holidays."

And (horrors!) VisitScotland has shrunk to the point where it is nothing more than a brochure and a website. The resorts provide all the information required by prospective visitors, and thanks to budget cutbacks, the tourism agency had to close 80 of its network of information centers.

IT DIDN'T STOP THERE

This initial scenario planning exercise was only the beginning. The idea was to make scenario thinking a continuous process at VisitScotland, and Ian Yeoman took the reins to help the organization envisage alternative futures that could emerge around some specific developments, such as:

- *War in Iraq.* Following September 11, 2001, military action in the Middle East looked inevitable. Would it have an impact on travel that would be felt in Scotland?

- *Foot-and-mouth disease.* How might the outbreak of this disease in Britain affect Scotland as a tourist destination?

- *Avian flu.* This epidemic originated in Asia, but thanks to air travel, it was spreading quickly to other parts of the world. What would it do to international travel? How would Scotland be affected?

Let's take a closer look at one of these three special planning sessions.

The Iraq War

As many of us were doing in 2002 and 2003, VisitScotland was closely watching the post–September 11 geopolitical drama as it was unfolding and was wondering what would happen and how future events might impact the Scottish tourism industry.

Executives at VisitScotland decided to conduct a scenario planning exercise specifically exploring the issue of a potential war on travel. A shorter time frame was chosen for this workshop—just five years—because this would allow the scenario builders to include a postwar recovery period in their thinking. (You can already see they were making certain assumptions about how long a conflict situation might last.) The scenarios were thus depicting the year 2008.

In the first round of analysis, Yeoman and the team worked out the two overarching uncertainties that would form the axes of a matrix. They began by identifying several driving forces that influence tourism, including business and consumer confidence, gross domestic product (GDP being a proxy for economic well-being), exchange rates, transportation possibilities, the price of oil (and thus the cost of transportation), levels of taxation (resulting in either more or less disposable income for tourists), consumer perceptions, media stories, and disruptions.

Again, too many factors to work with! Which ones were both highly uncertain and high-impact? The two main dimensions selected were, first, the nature of the disruption that would be caused by war, and second, economic behavior during those five years.

Each of these two important dimensions might develop in alternative ways, and the planners gave the outcomes very evocative labels.

First, the nature of the war's disruption. In this dimension, there were two alternative future outcomes:

"New Atlantis" implies widespread destruction, but at the end, a new order emerges and understanding prevails. "Balkans" would mean that the war would be long and protracted—and would essentially never end.

Second, economic behavior. In this dimension, there were also two alternative future outcomes:

As the name suggests, a mere "Hiccup" would mean that the war would be short and bring about a minimal impact on the economy. "Merchant of Doom," on the other hand, is not an economic scenario you would want to wake up to. Deep and painful for everyone, it practically implies an "end of the world as we know it" outcome.

Slapping these two dimensions together created a matrix with four scenarios, A, B, C and D as shown in the graphic.

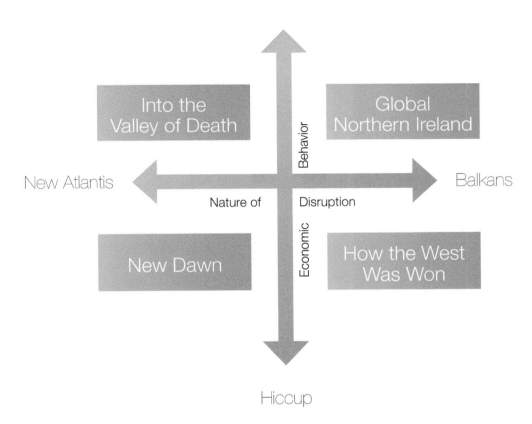

Merchant of Doom

Into the
Valley of Death

Global
Northern Ireland

New Atlantis

Behavior

Nature of　Disruption

Economic

Balkans

New Dawn

How the West
Was Won

Hiccup

Once again, the team gave the scenarios memorable names to convey what the four futures would look like and feel like. They fleshed out extremely detailed profiles of each scenario, from likely military developments to the thing they were all concerned about most: the impact on Scottish tourism.

Following are some excerpts from their highly imaginative—and in places, very prescient—report. (Keep in mind that these scenarios were created *before* the war had begun.)

SCENARIO: "GLOBAL NORTHERN IRELAND"

This scenario foresees that the war will be based on protracted military resistance. A high number of casualties will spark not only political difficulties, but also an antiwar movement and anti-American feelings worldwide. Iraq attacks oil facilities, causing major damage.

Meanwhile, terrorism spins out of control. Fear is the dominant emotion in 2008, as stock markets have plunged, unemployment continues to rise, and armed soldiers become an everyday part of the urban landscape.

Scenario Vignettes

"The prime minister ordered troops onto the streets of London. . . just a security measure, he said."

"It happened this morning, a bomb blast in Edinburgh that ripped through the lobby of [a] hotel. . . This was a daily occurrence all over the world. We now see troops stationed at Edinburgh airport, bomb scares, and security cordons."

"The worst day was on March 15, when the whole transport system came to a close. All regional airports were closed; it was as if nobody traveled that day. Roads saw no cars; railway stations were deserted. We all stayed at home that day."

"It's a situation of Big Brother, police state, and fear."

"[The war] backfired when bin Laden was immortalized as a martyr, leading to a series of world crusades between East and West, regional conflicts and flashpoints that hit the soft belly of aviation and tourism. People are now a lot more entrenched and cautious about things. It's about saving for tomorrow in case this world directly hits me."

"We have seen the US economy go to the brink of collapse, because it couldn't cope with the snowball effect of doom and gloom."

Impact on Tourism

- Tourism trips decline 4 percent in 2003, with a 4.5 percent decline in 2004; recovery does not begin until 2005.
- Scotland's reputation as a safe tourism destination is threatened.
- Certain tourism resorts in Scotland don't see any tourists in 2003.
- There's major disruption to international tourism as people stay at home or travel locally.
- Marketing activity focuses on visiting friends and relatives.
- Tourism retrenches for 2003 and 2004, as safety drives consumer choice.
- Value, safety, and service quality become hygiene factors in consumer choice.
- International hubs become the focus for disruption.
- Security costs become prohibitive in the short-haul European travel market.
- There's further consolidation in the airline sector, with many national carriers going bust.
- The propensity to travel is still there, but Scotland suffers due to the lack of direct air links.

SCENARIO: "HOW THE WEST WAS WON"

In a nutshell: We win. There is no terrorism activity and the whole thing turns out to be a small regional problem, a relatively minor blip in the grand scheme of things.

When the dust settles, economic growth and confidence return, and unemployment proves to have been a short-term problem.

Scenario Vignettes

"This was a war between the new generation and the precision of Western armaments on one hand, and clumsy World War I rifles and bayonets on the other. Saddam had no chance. It was all over in six months. I watched the movie via CNN. It was good watching."

"We had a minor economic blip; oil prices rose. Some short-term unemployment in the City (more like restructuring), old industries disappeared, and manufacturing was down slightly. That year's holiday was in Austria rather than Australia. But life went on as normal."

"One year later, confidence returned to the market. George Bush had saved the world. We had won. Nothing could beat us. Although there were continued regional hot spots, we had the Seventh Cavalry and could take anyone out. We all got used to increased security. It became part of the background. There was great prosperity, and we all lived happily ever after."

Impact on Tourism

- Tourism trips decline 0.5 percent overall.
- Overseas tourism is down.
- Business tourism is down.
- UK tourism grows.
- Scotland is a safe destination.
- Full recovery occurs in late 2003.
- It's a relatively normal year.
- Exchange rates are favorable for Scottish tourism; we see only moderate decline.
- Sharp recovery occurs in 2004.
- There's a sharp recovery in short-haul trips (one- to three-night holidays).
- Nonessential business trips are curtailed.
- Outbound travel to nations perceived as being at risk, especially those in North America, falls off.
- There's an increase in young families holidaying in Scotland.

SCENARIO: "NEW DAWN"

VisitScotland's third scenario foresaw a slower run-up to the outbreak of war—essentially an attempt to solve the Iraq situation through inspections and negotiations, but in the end, they fail. Iraq is attacked, and although Baghdad falls quickly, guerilla fighting (now a Holy War) continues in other parts of the country.

Saddam's one last shot is a chemical attack on Israel. This brings a tough response from the United States, in which Saddam is killed. This event marks the beginning of a new era for the Middle East, as world leaders work together to stabilize the region.

Scenario Vignettes

"One day, I remember President Bush addressed the nation. I will never forget that broadcast. It was one of those moments that you remember, like Princess Diana's death. Mr. Bush said that negotiations had broken down. In spite of the Iraqi leader having misled the UN diplomacy team, a major underground city complex near Tikrit had been discovered. Iraq was now refusing entry to the inspectors. In light of this failure to comply with the weapons inspections, the United States, with the support of the United Nations, had launched cruise missiles to take out the complex. This was the trigger to launch 'Baghdad First,' which was a strike at the heart of the Saddam Hussein regime, launching a fall from within."

"Although the price had been high for the final resolution, life continued at home, at least at first. Attempts at terrorist retaliation did continue for a while, causing some financial insecurity,

but they were without backing, and in this new climate they did not achieve much damage."

"Governments borrowed substantially, first to support recovery in Israel and Iraq, and then to promote peace in the Middle East. For this, those employed paid higher taxes and worked longer hours. We even saw many people continue to work into their 70s, because pension funds were unstable. It was now about tough economic decisions to bring resolution to this problem. The United Nations, led by the United States, became the vehicle for Middle East and world stability."

Impact on Tourism

- Overall tourism trips decline 3 percent.
- Average spending declines.
- There's a substantial decline in long-haul tourism.
- Short-haul European tourism is static.
- Domestic tourism increases.
- A budget carrier goes bust.
- International airports are seen as unsafe; land-based travel increases.
- Major holiday decisions are put off in 2003.
- Luxury and business tourism sectors see substantial turndown.
- Scotland is considered a safe destination.
- The cancellation of the Edinburgh Military Tattoo has major implications on international tourism.
- Budget accommodation is still robust and growing; there's a focus on "keep it simple" and "not over the top."
- Well-being and freedom holidays emerge as Scotland's strength.
- The family market remains strong.

SCENARIO: "INTO THE VALLEY OF DEATH"

In this final scenario, 350,000 American and British soldiers have died in Iraq; poisoning from chemical warfare has affected millions. Oil supplies come to a halt. Farm prices collapse and breadlines form in New York, where organized crime rules. The world is dealing with deflation, stock market collapse, banks going under, people's savings gone.

It does not sound like fun.

In fact, this scenario was so dire that VisitScotland decided to remove it from consideration and stick with the remaining three. As chief scenario planner Ian Yeoman says, "If the world economy collapsed into a 1930s-style depression, there would not be any point in marketing tourism, because very few people would be going on holiday."

Working with the Scenarios

Creating scenarios, especially ones as detailed as these, is not an exercise undertaken just to while away a few rainy hours in Edinburgh. They were meant to provide VisitScotland with insights and ideas that could guide business and policy decisions for the future.

It's worth mentioning that not everyone is always on board when it comes to scenario planning. To some people, the process seems like nothing more than writing scary bedtime stories for adults. That was the case here, according to Yeoman. The four war scenarios were at the stage where meat was being added to the bone, yet Yeoman was still having difficulty convincing some of his colleagues of the overall value of the exercise.

But as the tensions in Iraq continued to mount, the planning group began to witness certain elements of the scenarios they had just been developing actually coming true. "The pivotal point," Yeoman recalls, "was when Tony Blair announced that British troops would be stationed at Heathrow Airport. Seeing these soldiers on television dramatically shifted senior stakeholders' perception of the problem." This scene—straight out of "Global Northern Ireland"—opened the eyes of the skeptics and actually spurred the group on to an even more intense round of scenario planning afterward.

When the scenarios had been finished and qualitatively validated, they were given to Oxford Economics Forecasting, an econometrics consultancy, to quantify the impact of each one. OEF assessed the effect of the three story lines on travel to Scotland from within the United Kingdom, from overseas, as well as on short break and business travel segments of the tourism market.

Following a detailed analysis, OEF came to the conclusion that a short, decisive war in Iraq might not be so detrimental to Scottish tourism. Perceived as safe, the country would benefit from travelers from the rest of the United Kingdom, who might prefer to take short breaks in Scotland rather than abroad.

Of course, the actual situation would be complex, and there would be many offsetting factors. If the "Global Northern Ireland" scenario emerged, the United Kingdom would enter a recession, and some of the money that would have been spent on travel would dry up.

Still, having the scenarios in hand gave the tourism authorities a certain sense of comfort that they were more in control, and when the war did break out, there was no sense of panic but rather a cool-headed responsiveness that prevailed. A joint action group was established, and this team successfully coordinated the response of Scottish tourism to what was going on, particularly with regard to getting the communication right with the public and other industry players. The focus was on providing useful information rather than passing on one message after another of doom and gloom—the kind of communication that was starting to appear everywhere.

At the same time, they also set up a process to monitor booking patterns and consumer and business confidence, so they would have their finger on the pulse of any changes that would affect the sector.

WHAT ACTUALLY PLAYED OUT?

As is often the case, as reality unfolds it turns out to reflect a *blend* of the scenarios created, rather than being an exact fit with only one of them. The Iraq War was no exception. Although militarily, "How the West Was Won" comes closest to describing how things panned out in reality, terrorism has still not been vanquished. Our daily lives are still affected by issues raised in "Global Northern Ireland"—fear, "Big Brother," and security. Nowhere is this more evident than when we travel.

With a clearer understanding of these issues, thanks in part to the thoroughness of the scenario planning exercise, VisitScotland was able to identify some vulnerabilities to be aware of and prepare for:

- The American market, traditionally Scotland's largest overseas source of tourist arrivals, could decline because of Americans' perceptions of security, sensitivity to anti-American sentiments, a weakening economy, and an unfavorable exchange rate. In terms of marketing effort, continental Europeans could be a better target audience. They might be attracted to Scotland for short-break vacations, and they would be less susceptible to exchange rate weaknesses that turn Scotland into an expensive destination.

- International hubs such as Heathrow and Gatwick are important gateways for many visitors to Scotland, but since they may continue to be prime targets for terrorism, travelers transiting those two airports are likely to face many security-related inconveniences. (And God forbid there would actually be a terrorist attack at one of these airports, but if there would be, Scotland would clearly experience a disruption.) VisitScotland should therefore lobby for more direct flights to Scotland, bypassing the hubs.

- As geopolitical tensions push up the price of oil, Scottish tourism will also be affected. Cheap flights may not be so cheap any more. Travel by car will also be more expensive. To alleviate this vulnerability, Scotland could promote public transportation and help develop alternatives. And, as Ian Yeoman notes, Scotland's remote islands would benefit from electric cars rather than those running on gasoline.

- Increased terrorist activity in Europe could cause the United Kingdom to introduce tougher entry requirements for visitors, such as visas, and this additional hoop to jump through could be enough, when added to all the other inconveniences of travel, to prevent some visitors from planning a vacation in Scotland. What could VisitScotland do about this? Lobby for more sensible solutions.

Last, one of the key values of scenario planning in this context has been that it serves as a reminder to the tourism authorities in Scotland that they need to spend time gaining a realistic understanding of the threats that could affect them, so they can formulate appropriate contingency and communication plans if unfavorable scenarios do materialize.

Welcome to Scotland
Fàilte gu Alba

"Even if you're on the right track, you'll get **run over** if you just sit there."

Will Rogers

CHAPTER 4

BLACK SWANS

There's an ancient Chinese proverb, "No battle plan ever survives contact with the enemy." Earlier in my career, I used to make sure this phrase was added to the cover page whenever I produced a marketing or strategic plan—unless, that is, I didn't think my boss at the time would be receptive to a little sardonic humor before he had even read the table of contents. Not every CEO would appreciate the idea this quotation was meant to convey, namely:

> Yes, boss, here's my plan, but please don't expect us to be able to execute it in every detail. Why not? Because as the year progresses, we're bound to learn more about things going on in our markets, understand our customers better than we do right now, and, with luck, identify one or two interesting new opportunities that happen to come along. We'll also find out how our competitors will react to what we're doing. And last, along the way, we're sure to be confronted with some unforeseen events, too. In other words, contact with the enemy (or, to use the layman's term, *reality*) means that our plan (excellent though it may be!) might have to be revised on the fly.

"Unforeseen events"—now there's a phrase to fill the heart of any strategic planner with dread! Even if your plan creatively takes into account a range of well-thought-out future scenarios, you can't avoid the possibility that something totally unexpected will come out of left field and, in one fell swoop, render your vision obsolete—along with all that hard work you put into the plan.

At least, that is what some planners think, and they're not altogether wrong. But they're not altogether right, either. Scenario planning can't predict unforeseen events; that much is certain. But it can help you if and when they do occur. We'll look at the how and why in a moment, but for now, let's look more closely at the concept of an "unforeseen event."

Required Reading

In scenario planning, these unexpected occurrences that come along and ruin your plan, if not your whole day, are usually called *wild cards* or *black swans*. Let's use this latter term, which comes from one of the best business books to be written in the past 10 years, *The Black Swan* by Nassim Nicholas Taleb.

In this fascinating and challenging book, Taleb describes a black swan event as one that has three main characteristics. First, it's extremely rare or has only a tiny probability of happening. It is something that's considered so unlikely, so far beyond the range of realistic expectations, that it's simply disregarded as a possibility.

In fact, the name "black swan" mirrors this mentality. Since Roman times, a black swan was a concept posited by philosophers to represent something that cannot exist. Their assumption, based on observing swans in the real world, was that all swans must be white. (Their assumption was valid right up to 1790, when a species of black swan was discovered by an English explorer in Australia.)

A slightly different kind of black swan is an event that is not considered so rare that you don't need to waste time quantifying its probability, but one that is entirely inconceivable in the first place. This type of black swan is literally unpredictable.

Both of these kinds of events—the one you know could happen but dismiss because of its minuscule probability, and the one you have no idea could happen at all—have one thing in common: When they do happen, they take you by surprise.

Taleb's second condition for a black swan event is that, if it does happen, it has an enormous, disproportionate impact. It's not just an important event; it's a game changer. What exactly that means depends on you and your game. Certain black swans could have huge, long-term consequences that reach right around the globe. For example, the rise of Facebook could scarcely have been predicted a dozen years ago, but since its launch, it has changed the way hundreds of millions of people communicate and interact.

Not every black swan is a global game changer, though. The impact of the event could be limited to only your own organization or industry, virtually unnoticed and unfelt by anybody else. But in spite of its narrow scope, it is still a black swan if it has a profound effect on the people and organizations it touches. Say you own a grocery store, for example. All is well until, one day, Walmart enters your market. Walmart? How is that possible? You always believed your town was too small for Walmart! Yet here it comes. You (and most other retailers in town) are stunned; for you, this is a classic black swan event—one that was never expected but now will change your business fortunes completely. For the businesses that don't compete with Walmart, though, life pretty much goes on as usual. The arrival of the retail giant has no major implications, so for them, it's not a black swan at all.

Taleb's third factor (in my opinion, the least important of the three) is that after the black swan event has occurred, people look back and claim it all made sense; it wasn't really so surprising after all.

There are two other points worth making about black swans. You might conclude that such events happen in a sudden burst—like a business Vesuvius that wipes out its competitors like so many unsuspecting Pompeians. But not always. Taleb himself mentions the rise of the Internet as a black swan, and as we all know, the Internet didn't get big overnight. What's crucial is not how fast the Internet's impact was felt but how far-reaching it eventually proved to be.

There is also the matter of perspective to consider. Taleb illustrates this point with the life of a turkey. Month after month, the turkey is very well fed and looked after by a kindly farmer. Who could blame the bird for thinking he's got it made? Comfortable life, plenty of food. . . and extrapolating from the past, the turkey makes the logical assumption that this wonderful, cushy life will go on forever.

It doesn't. To his complete surprise, the day before Thanksgiving he's taken out behind the woodshed and. . . well, you get the idea. From the turkey's viewpoint, a more dramatic black swan event could hardly be imagined.

From the farmer's vantage point, however, everything simply proceeded according to plan. He spent a year fattening the turkey in preparation for that sumptuous Thanksgiving dinner with all the fixings. When the time came, the final phase of the plan called for the turkey's demise. So that's what happened. For the farmer, this was a turkey tale, not a black swan saga.

Events, Dear Boy! Events!

In a famous interview from the 1950s, Prime Minister Harold Macmillan of the United Kingdom was praised for the thoroughness of his government agenda by a journalist who then asked, "But is there anything, sir, that you think could blow it all off course?"

The prime minister's famous reply: "Events, dear boy! Events!"

Just so. The unexpected can change everything. But that doesn't mean that you have to resign yourself to being completely derailed if something unforeseen comes along. For your organization, one of the big benefits of scenario planning is that it not only helps you see the general outlines of a number of different futures that may come to pass, but in doing so it also improves the mental agility of your management team, preparing them to think in terms of unusual possibilities—even thinking about the unthinkable. So when an unforeseen event does occur, it will come less as a surprise and more as a challenge to be addressed and taken in stride.

A Few Black Swans throughout History

A *black swan* is an event that is not predicted in advance and yet, when it occurs, has an enormous effect. As Taleb describes these events, they always come as a surprise. But after the fact, you look back and, seeing the logic of how they developed, are convinced that actually they were foreseeable all along.

Collectively, probably 99 percent of the arc of human history can be attributed to these types of unexpected occurrences—events, inventions, and discoveries that no one imagined before they happened, and after they did happen, the world was not the same again. Some of these black swans loom so large that the timeline of history is divided between the "preevent" world and the "postevent" world. The post–black swan situation is then considered a "new normal."

Following are a few examples.

WORLD WAR I

As June 1914 began, none of the leaders in London, Paris, Berlin, or Saint Petersburg could have imagined that at the end of that very month, an assassination in Sarajevo, an insignificant Balkan town they might have been hard-pressed to locate on a map, would trigger a sequence of ultimatums and mobilizations that within a few days would plunge the whole continent, and then the world, into the Great War. Yet today, any History 101 professor worth his or her salt can explain the rush to war as if it were all inevitable, the easy-to-understand consequence of trends such as the rise of nationalism in Europe, the complex tangle of alliances in place, and the arms race between England and Germany. The impact of this black swan was titanic: an entire generation decimated; the map of Europe, Africa, and the Middle East redrawn; the rise of fascism; and, eventually, World War II.

SEPTEMBER 11, 2001

Vague intelligence reports hinted at what was to come, but despite the strident insistence by some people that it should have been possible to connect the dots and prevent the terrorist attacks by four hijacked planes in the United States, it was in fact impossible to predict that awful day in any practical sense before it actually happened. The immediate impact on the economy, and its profound geopolitical consequences, are still felt today, not to mention the permanent changes 9/11 brought about in the security gauntlet we all have to run whenever we travel by air. The new normal is not very nice.

LEHMAN BROTHERS BANKRUPTCY AND THE 2008 FINANCIAL CRISIS

In an interview on the shortcomings of forecasting, Peter Brabeck, former CEO of Nestlé, remarked, "I am not aware of any bank in the world that predicted the financial crisis in its multiyear plan. And yet, for the entire banking industry, this crisis was by far the most seismic event that has occurred in the last few years." Yet, when you look back at the sequence of events that led to the crisis, it all seems so logical and predictable, doesn't it?

2010 GULF OF MEXICO OIL SPILL

Industries whose livelihood depended on the condition of the Gulf of Mexico's waters (e.g., the local fishing and tourism industries) learned what a black swan was about on April 20 of that year, when an offshore oil rig fire cascaded into a catastrophic spill. Eventually, almost 5 million barrels of oil were released into the sea, with economic and environmental damage estimated as high as $100 billion. Was it predictable? Experts familiar with the rig's operation knew that some risks were being taken; maybe they could have foreseen the accident and imagined its consequences. But people living their day-to-day lives onshore would not have imagined it. A classic black swan scenario.

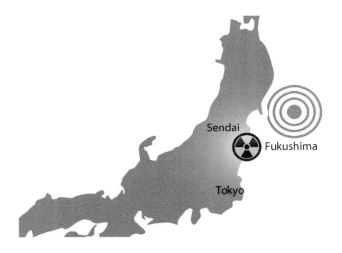

2011 JAPANESE TSUNAMI

One of the most powerful earthquakes ever recorded (magnitude 9.0) triggered a disastrous tsunami on Japan's northeast coast, with enormous damage to property and heavy loss of life. But in addition to the local human tragedy, the disaster was also a calamitous black swan event for the entire world's nuclear energy industry: Seawater flooded the Fukushima nuclear power plant and the fuel rods melted down. Practically overnight, opposition to nuclear energy started regaining international momentum after years of relative quiescence. Within three months, Switzerland, Germany, and Italy had all renounced atomic power as a future energy source, and many other countries were debating its safety risks. At this writing, the future for this industry looks very bleak.

POSITIVE BLACK SWAN EVENTS

Based on these examples, you could be forgiven for believing that a black swan is an event that by its nature has a negative impact. That's not always the case, though! Think of technological progress, for example. Often, leaps in technology or medicine come about because of a black swan–type discovery.

A good example of this is the discovery of penicillin and the subsequent development of modern antibiotics. Hardly anyone today (outside of the world's poorest countries) dies of infectious diseases, let alone gets a scratch and dies from infection. Yet before antibiotics, this happened all the time. In every war up to World War II, more casualties were caused by infection than actual battle wounds. Sir Alexander Fleming and his miraculous discovery changed everything.

The accidental discovery of the New World is another example of a positive black swan event that no one predicted but that, obviously, changed the entire course of history.

Of course, on a microlevel, black swan events happen in our own lives, too. Think of the probabilities that came into play when you met the man or woman you eventually married. The how-I-met-your-mother stories we tell our kids are perfect examples of those improbable, one-in-a-million encounters that end up having significant consequences. "I missed my train so I decided to wait for the next one at the little café around the corner. There I was, drinking my coffee and minding my own business when in walks the most beautiful woman I ever saw. . . "

Tiny probability. Huge impact!

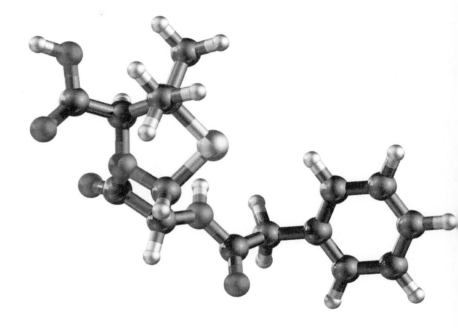

What If…?

What if the United States announced that anyone with a university degree, from any country in the world, could automatically receive a green card and come live and work in America, starting tomorrow?

What if France changed the language of instruction in its entire education system to English in order to make French citizens more globally competitive?

What if little green men from Mars came to Earth and gave humanity the gift of limitless free, clean energy?

These three made-up events are all extremely unlikely. (I admit, France switching to English is about as far-fetched as you can get.) But I'm sure you would also agree that if they ever did occur, there would be consequences for many industries and companies in America as well as the rest of the world, perhaps yours among them. That's the essence of the black swan event: low probability, high impact.

What good are these black swans? Can you actually *do* anything with them?

Yes. After you've defined and described a set of future scenarios, and a flexible strategy is starting to take shape, it's a valuable exercise—and a very interesting one—to subject it to a few off-the-wall what-if questions to see how well it holds up. This isn't because these what-ifs might actually come to pass (although in theory they could), but rather to stress-test your strategy, to see whether it can accommodate the unexpected. It also gives the brains of the members of your scenario planning group a good workout.

Some scenario planners call these extreme tests *wild cards*, but we'll stick to black swans here. The objective is to ensure your strategy will have the resilience and agility that will allow your organization to deal with surprises and potential body blows.

Accordingly, most black swans revolve around serious risks your company may suddenly face—existential risks, even. You would normally stress-test your strategy with a black swan situation straight out of *Tales of the Four Horsemen of the Apocalypse*: Could it withstand a war or natural disaster that disrupted supply chains or affected your markets? What would be the impact of a SARS-like epidemic? What if your biggest customer went bust? Or worse, sued you for all you're worth?

The positive black swans sound less dire, but even very fortuitous market events may have unexpected consequences as time goes on, so they are worth thinking about as well. Free energy from those incredibly generous Martians is not an existential threat (unless you're in the energy business yourself, of course), but thinking about the consequences of competing in a world where the cost of energy has dropped to zero is not only a cool thought experiment that will undoubtedly stretch minds and generate some fascinating ideas, but could help you see how competition would change in your business if this constraint were removed. In the real world, it might never be removed, but it could play less of a role some day.

Nevertheless, the kind of black swans you will want to focus on are the ones that could put your company six feet underground, either because they threaten you specifically and directly, or because they threaten the health and stability of your industry as a whole—or the entire economy, in which case your company would find itself in a struggle to survive.

Examples of the first kind of black swan would be:

- A powerful competitor launches a product superior to your own— something so much better that you could be wiped off the map.
- You unexpectedly lose key talent (a team defects to another company, something dire happens to the management, etc.).
- A new regulation forces you to change the way you do business, at huge cost to your bottom line.
- A major industrial accident occurs.

In the second category, there are countless horrific possibilities that could befall the world and affect you in a negative way. I already mentioned war and pestilence, but very unpleasant outcomes could also result from other occurrences. Here are just a few examples:

- The US dollar is dropped as the world's reserve currency, or the euro collapses.
- Your most critical raw material suddenly skyrockets in price.
- The corporate tax rate is hiked significantly.
- The stock market crashes.

"Now wait just a gosh-darn minute," you're saying. "If a black swan is unpredictable, how can anybody just sit down and make up a list of them? Once it's been predicted, how can it still be a black swan?"

That is correct. These aren't really black swans in the sense of being absolutely unimaginable events (seeing as how I've just imagined them).

Rather, they're just a few examples of the kinds of events that could derail even the best strategy. Stretch your thinking and come up with your own, especially ones that are specific to your own organization's vulnerabilities. After exploring what the consequences could be for your strategy, you'll be in a better position to add in the elements needed to ensure its robustness.

“ There is **nothing** about
a caterpillar that tells you
it's going to be a butterfly. ”

Buckminster Fuller

CHAPTER 5

ARE YOU READY?

I love reading books about the fascinating new world that the future has in store for us, don't you? My study is full of them, and Amazon.com loves me because I'm always ordering more. I'm intrigued and genuinely impressed by all the insightful predictions of how we'll be living our lives 20 years from now. . . or 50. Flying cars! Pills to make you smarter! World peace!

One book I recently read was bold enough to describe the future 100 years from now. (I'm not so sure I'll be around to find out if it's accurate.)

Predicting the future is sexy. In principle, though, scenario planners shouldn't do it. We should try to visualize what *could* happen and avoid acting as if we know what *will* happen, because, honestly, we don't. Besides, the main value of scenario planning lies in describing a *range* of futures, not pointing to one particularly glamorous prognosis with a "Stand back, everybody, this is it!" mind-set.

With that caveat, this part of the book is about the future, but without the confident, absolute predictions you might find in the best sellers stacked high on my desk. Instead, I'll highlight just a handful of trends that are going on now, all of which beg the provocative question, "Where could this lead? What kind of world could emerge if these developments continue?"

Zeroing in on the driving forces shaping our future, most trend watchers focus on the political, economic, societal, and technological (PEST) changes that are happening (or, if you recall from Chapter 2 of the book, STEBNPDILE) and how they will affect us. Instead of covering all these bases, in the next few pages I've selected some trends going on that may have an indirect, longer-term impact on us *as people*—as consumers and also as a society (the *S* in PEST). The *P*, *E*, and *T* elements of the model can wait for the sequel.

Why the focus on *S*? Because societal changes are the murkiest to imagine, but arguably the most far-reaching in the long term. In a sense, they are the "consequences of the consequences" of some other kind of trend.

For example, take the precipitous rise in the price of oil. That's clearly an economic trend—and obviously a very important one. One of its many consequences (a no-brainer as far as predictions go) could be that very high gasoline prices at the pump would force middle-class consumers down a notch or two as far as their personal transportation is concerned. To ease the burden on their family budget, bigger car owners would trade in their cars for smaller, more efficient cars, and lower-income families might have to give up their cars altogether and take the bus. (We've seen that movie before, in fact, back in the 1970s.) So the direct economic consequence of the oil situation has to do with the car industry and public transportation, and perhaps with the growth axes of cities in the future. But one of the consequences of the consequences could also be a steadily rising resentment on the part of the new "have-nots" toward the "still-haves" who can continue to drive their luxury cars and SUVs (which are now considered ostentatious objects of derision and envy).

Resentment, envy, anger—these are attitudes that could play out in many ways, not all of them pleasant. So the rising price of oil could end up having interesting repercussions on society's attitudes toward disparities in wealth. Ultimately, changing attitudes can have a critically important effect on consumer behavior and politics—and therefore on all kinds of companies and organizations.

The idea in these next few pages is to get you to think about these indirect connections, then look at your company and ask yourself whether you are ready.

Demographics: The War for Talent

Compared to new technologies or rapidly rising commodity prices, demographic changes are glacially slow to work their way through a population, which makes them easy for the person on the street to overlook. Yet, imperceptible as these trends may be, they potentially have a bigger and longer-lasting impact than almost any other kind of change.

A lot has been written about the aging populations in the developed world, a phenomenon that's inexorably coming about thanks to two trends: ever lower fertility rates (i.e., fewer babies being born) and increased longevity. There are myriad consequences of the trend toward an older population, ranging from increased health care costs to a shift in Florida's evening rush hour as retirees pile into their cars and head out en masse for their "early-bird dinners" at 4:30 in the afternoon.

Let's focus on just one of the consequences here—the one that could have an important impact on any organization that's concerned about its competitiveness over the next decade. (That should cover just about everybody.)

Over the past generation birthrates have been falling, so right about now, we are starting to see the effect of this trend on the labor pool in many countries, and the outlook is not very pretty. Fewer and fewer babies born, starting 20 years ago, means fewer and fewer young adults entering the workforce, starting today. Take Germany as an example. Because of the huge number of babies that were not born over the past two decades, the German labor pool is expected to shrink by a staggering 5 million people in the next 10 to 15 years. Other countries are facing a similarly dire situation.

At the same time, with more retirees leaving the labor pool to collect their pension checks, and fewer younger people entering it and paying toward the cost of those pensions, a page-one-screaming-headline type of financial crisis is looming. The countries that are at the bleeding edge of this problem may have little choice but to raise the age of retirement, increase taxes, cut pensions, cut other state-provided services—or all of these.

The mere threat of this happening has already caused rioting in Greece. But when it actually happens, some countries may become dark and nasty places in which to try to make a living. The business environment will be awful. Taxes will be high, and the underground economy will metastasize. Education and essential services may suffer from cutbacks. Social and labor unrest, unemployment, increased security issues—you name it—problems like these will be on your doorstep.

It doesn't sound like the land of opportunity, does it? And sure enough, many younger people, especially those with an education and decent prospects in life, might pack up and leave, emigrating in search of a place where jobs are more plentiful, the streets are safer, and they, and eventually their kids, have a chance for a better future. Think it couldn't happen? Over a million people emigrated from Russia in the past 20 years, and the bloom of Ireland's young men and women are leaving for Britain and Australia right now. We live in a mobile world.

What does it mean for a country to be losing population like this?

For one thing, it means that *competition for talent* is going to heat up. In the aggregate, companies that hire young graduates are going to be facing an ever-smaller pool of candidates. Since the law of supply and demand applies to the market for talent just as it applies to any other resource, the price of talent is going to go up. Are you ready for this?

For many organizations (maybe yours, if you're lucky), this may not be a problem. Your employment package may be so attractive that you will be turning good people away. Bully for you! But it's a zero-sum game. The numbers are already clear: There won't be enough talent to go around. Some companies will be winners. Some will be losers. Companies that aren't competitive in their ability to attract, hire, and retain the talent they want will find themselves losing the war for talent. What then?

Questions:

Do you have a strategy to ensure that you are one of the winners and not one of the losers in this critical arena? Or, if you believe you can't afford to be a winner, do you have an alternative strategy you can implement?

China's Bare Branches

The economic rise of China is the big story of the past 20 years. Could China's unexpected stagnation and decline be the big story of the *next* 20?

If such a scenario would come to pass, it could be because China faces two huge demographic challenges today that could undercut its ability to keep on growing before serious social problems get in the way.

The first challenge is that China's population is aging extraordinarily quickly. Other developed countries are all aging as well, but China is undergoing a particularly speedy transformation to an old society. This is thanks to its infamous one-child population control policy, introduced at the end of the 1970s. Limiting urban couples to only one child, the policy has been very successful on its face: It has cut fertility dramatically and prevented about 300 million births over the past 30 years—the equivalent of the entire population of the United States.

But beware the law of unintended consequences, especially when it comes to social engineering! Stop 300 million people from being born, and—*quelle surprise*—you begin to seriously distort your population structure. China's average age is skewing higher and higher, with the ratio of elderly dependents to people still in the labor force increasing very fast. By the year 2030, the country will actually have more dependents than children.

In China, elderly people have traditionally been taken care of by their children. But thanks to the one-child policy, people there now speak of the "4–2–1 formula": An only child will have two parents and four grandparents to look after.

The result: China can expect many of its older people to be institutionalized. There simply won't be enough young people to look after the older generation in the traditional way. Could this be a market opportunity? Sure. In fact, now might be a good time to invest in companies offering services aimed at assisted living for the elderly. But what will be the cost in terms of China's social cohesion and values?

However, the looming problems of the elderly are not the only demographic challenge the country is facing. In the next decade, it could also have to deal with the even more far-reaching consequences of its second big problem, which the Chinese are calling "bare branches."

For centuries, Chinese culture (like others in Asia) has valued girls less than boys. Particularly in rural areas, couples want a boy, who can contribute some muscle around the farm, helping to work the land with his father.

But since the advent of the one-child policy, if a couple's first child is a girl, there is, officially, no second chance for a boy. (In certain provinces, the government magnanimously permits couples a second child if their first-born is a girl.) For some couples, this means that if they can control the sex of their child, they will do what it takes to make sure the one child they are allowed will be a boy. And they *do* have control. If prenatal testing confirms that their unborn child is a girl, they can abort the baby. In extreme cases, particularly in the countryside, newborn girls may even be abandoned to die immediately after they are born, with no record made of a birth at all. In short, it is possible to ensure that you don't have a living daughter, which leaves you free to try again for a son.

To be sure, both sex-selective abortion and infanticide are banned in China. But they happen anyway. In one survey, more than a third of the women who had had abortions admitted they did so in order to select the sex of their baby. (Read: Only girls were aborted.)

The result? China has a male-to-female sex ratio that is extraordinarily male-heavy. Countrywide, for every 100 female births reported, there are 119 male births. In some provinces this ratio is as high as 135 boys to 100 girls. No natural explanation is possible for a ratio as high as this.

If you look only at the segment of China's population under age 20, there are 30 million more males than females. Such a huge imbalance has potentially momentous consequences for China's future, as millions of Chinese men have no hope of being able to find a wife and start a family, at least not with a Chinese woman. It really redefines the notion of a divide between haves and have-nots.

These unlucky young men are called "bare branches" in China: They're like the branches of a tree that will never bear fruit.

Questions:

In all of human history, there has never been a phenomenon quite like this. Where could it lead? How might Chinese society—and the government—try to remedy this situation? Through emigration? Mail-order brides? Channeling all that pent-up energy into military adventures? What kind of economic impact could this imbalance (or its solution) have? If your company does business in China, are there consequences for you?

Urbanization: The Big Grab

Say good-bye to the world of cheap energy and raw materials that we've known and loved over the past couple of generations. Although there will be the usual ups and downs along the way, the overall trend line as the future unfolds could be one of steadily rising commodity and energy prices.

In the good old days, it was mainly supply issues and constraints that determined commodity prices. They were affected by such things as harvests and hurricanes, wars and work stoppages—events that had an impact on supply, or at least on the reliability of distribution. A few years ago, to use oil as an example, OPEC could turn the supply tap on or off, controlling oil prices fairly closely.

Supply constraints and disruptions are still important, but they've been overshadowed by the sheer power of demand to bid prices higher. This demand is largely the result of the emergence of a new middle class in the developing world, soon comprising about 1 billion people worldwide. India alone is expecting a dramatic surge in the size of its middle class, from 5 percent of its total population in 2005 to 41 percent in 2025—that's an increase of 550 million new consumers. In China, the urban population will grow by nearly 300 million people between now and the year 2025, most of that being middle-class growth.

Increased urbanization and increased consumerism are the twin motors that could drive commodity price increases for many years to come. Urbanization means greater demand for infrastructure and housing, while consumerism means more demand for durable goods such as cars, refrigerators, TVs, air conditioners, and the many other energy-consuming appliances that Western households have taken for granted for years. Producing more of this infrastructure, plus all the other goodies demanded by the newly affluent, would require more steel, more copper, more rubber, more timber, more cement. . . and, of course, more energy.

Take cars, for example. China recently overtook Japan to become the world's second-largest market (after the United States) for new cars. Over the next decade, the number of privately owned cars on the road in China is forecasted to increase from 25 to 140 million. (I calculate that to park all those 115 million new cars, you'd need a lot measuring 19 miles long by 19 miles wide.) Thomas Friedman, in his book *The World Is Flat*, notes that in Beijing alone, 30,000 new cars were being added to the roads each month—1,000 *every day*.

With more cars comes demand for more gasoline, so we can expect oil prices to increase steadily as well. Many observers think a price tag of $200 a barrel is a realistic possibility in the next few years. But even at $200, there could still be too much demand and/or too little supply.

Questions:

What could be the consequences of significantly higher oil prices? Higher inflation, as prices reflect higher transport costs? Pressure on such industries as travel and tourism? Political tensions? Or could the political will finally emerge to do what it takes to bring profitable alternative energy sources onstream more quickly?

GOBBLING UP THE WORLD'S RAW MATERIALS

China's galloping economic growth, coupled with its rapid urbanization, could mean that the country's ravenous hunger for building materials, energy, food, and consumer goods will continue for the foreseeable future. To put it bluntly: China could gobble up the lion's share of the world's basic raw materials.

According to Barclays Capital, China already consumes a quarter of the world's copper, compared with a tenth a decade ago. It accounts for more than 90 percent of the global growth in demand for aluminum. It also accounts for about 10 percent of global oil demand, up from just 3 percent 20 years ago.

In fact, China's appetite for these commodities is so huge that the country's foreign policy revolves around its relentless need to secure supplies of oil and other natural resources. In 2007, China's president Hu went on a natural resources shopping safari across the continent of Africa, resulting in such deals as a 45 percent stake in a Nigerian offshore oil block and an arrangement to mine $12 billion worth of copper ore in Congo—a sum that happens to be more than three times Congo's annual budget.

China is also investing in oil exploration and mining opportunities in Canada, Venezuela, and Peru, and sugar refining in Australia. It lends money to Russia and Brazil in exchange for commodities it needs.

Questions:

Will China's hunger for raw materials and agricultural commodities continue? If so, can we expect that world prices will be pushed higher and higher? Could they lock up the supply of key commodities, leaving nothing for anyone else? Money talks, but could there eventually be a political backlash to selling such huge quantities of important resources to the Chinese?

WE'RE HUNGRY!

The "next billion" also want to eat better. Rising incomes mean improving diets, especially more meat consumption. A decade from now, the world's total meat consumption is expected to be about 65 percent higher than it was 20 years ago.

To meet the increased demand for meat and other foodstuffs, the world's agricultural production would need to crank up significantly. But that may not be easy, for several reasons. Biofuel production (thanks to misplaced political incentives) has already shifted a good-sized portion of the world's agricultural commodities out of the food chain and into energy production. Urbanization has also reduced available acreage in many markets, and the amount of arable land per capita is dropping. It's not just the quantity of land that's needed for agriculture that's an issue; the quality of land is critical as well. If it isn't high enough, yields may be lower. Fertilizer supplies are also a factor in production. Irrigation can be an issue as well, so water supply and prices also have to be factored in.

Meanwhile, the politicization of agricultural markets could continue. Rice is a good example. Panic over high prices in 2007 and 2008 led some countries (e.g., India, Thailand, Japan, Indonesia, Vietnam, and China) to restrict exports in an attempt to counter domestic inflation and ease potential unrest over shortages. But all this accomplished was to drive global prices even higher.

For you and me, higher food prices would be an inconvenience. But for the hundreds of millions of people in the world who already spend most of their disposable income on food, it could be a disaster. It may also be a disaster for the governments in the parts of the world where these people live, because food shortages cause instability. It was food price inflation that sparked the initial unrest in Tunisia and Egypt, for example, leading to deposed leaders within weeks.

Questions:

What other countries could be vulnerable to a rise in the price of basic foodstuffs? How could their governments react? If food prices continue to climb, could we see calls for intervention in the markets on humanitarian grounds—resulting in more artificially induced price distortion? Could biofuel subsidies be cut? What impact could that have on the price of food (and fuel)?

When 90 Is the New 60

Our life spans are getting longer—much longer. For most of human history, people lived to the ripe old age of about 30. Globally speaking, it's only been in the past century that our life expectancy took off. The world average in 2010 was 67.2 years, although like all averages, this figure masks some dismally low life expectancies (e.g., below 50 years in several parts of Africa).

Thanks to medical advances and healthier living, our longevity is extending. If the trend continues, some scientists think half the babies born in the developed world will live to celebrate their hundredth birthday.

Living to 100 would be great, right? Well, maybe. As Jay Leno once said, the problem with living longer is that you get those extra years when you're in your 80s, when what you *really* want is some extra years when you're in your 20s.

This trend to longer life spans will no doubt have several interesting societal consequences, some of which may already start affecting us in the next dozen years.

One of these could be that we will change the way we order, or segment, our lives. To understand what I mean, imagine that 100 years becomes a common lifespan but that nothing else changes in our lives. Say that, as now, you spend the first few years of your life in school and college, completing your formal education at age 22. Is it even conceivable that this education will still be relevant to you 60, 70, almost 80 years later?

As today, you start your professional career after the education phase is over, and retire at (let's say) age 65. Then what? Putter around the garden, take ballroom dancing lessons, and do Sudoku for 35 years?

Looking at your career, if it, too, follows today's normal trajectory, you would tend to stay in the same profession for the 40 or so years of your working life. If you're good at what you do, you will rise up through the ranks of the organizations employing you, but this movement is generally upward, rarely into an entirely new field. If you start out as an architect, it would be unusual to become a corporate lawyer or high school biology teacher. If you're trained as a cook, you will probably not switch to glass-blowing or industrial design.

If then, as now, you marry at around age 27 or 28, would you and your partner really stay together for 72 years?

These notions may not make much sense in the years to come.

NEW RETIREMENT PLAN:
WORK TILL YOU'RE 80

The concept of paying retirees a pension first appeared in the 1880s when Chancellor Otto von Bismarck set out to build the world's first welfare state in newly united Germany. He introduced a tax on workers to finance a modest annuity that would allow old people a chance to decline in dignity at the end of their lives. But that was the key to this idea: The payments would ease *the end of their lives*. The age when the payments kicked in (initially 70, later reduced to 65) was very close to the average life expectancy.

Bismarck understood that the most logical age for retirement would be when people near the end of their productive lives. In the 1880s, this meant age 65. He could never have dreamed that pension payments might one day have to be made to retirees for 35 years.

Is the age of retirement sacrosanct? Nowadays, people are not used up at age 65—far from it. In the US Senate, for example, 39 percent of the

100 senators are over age 65. Eleven are over 75. (Sometimes it seems as if all 100 are senile, though, so maybe this is not a good group to use as an example.)

Questions:

Over the next generation, could we see our official working lives stretching from the current 40 years (age 25 to 65) to 55 or 60 years in length? This means we'd be working well into our 80s—but the age of retirement would be in line with our longer productive lives. Is this realistic from a political point of view? What if it doesn't happen? Financially, there could be a huge shortfall as Social Security funds dry up, paying for more retirees who live longer and stay on the government's dime much longer. Could there be a backlash against "unproductive" older people? Could retirees who elect to spend three decades dawdling about at government expense be stigmatized by society—or at least by the younger workers shouldering the financial burden? In such a case, could it be, "Farewell, class warfare; hello, generational warfare"?

BACK TO SCHOOL

As fast as our know-how is accelerating, it seems absurd to expect that an education completed when you're in your early 20s won't be obsolete by the time you're 40, let alone 80. In some technical fields, what you learn in the first year of a four-year curriculum is already out of date by the time you graduate!

In the next few years, forward-thinking educators could succeed in convincing governments, teachers' unions, and parents that our present educational model is not sustainable and begin a major overhaul of the education industry: how it's structured; what it's meant to achieve; and how, when, and by whom it's delivered (more on this subject in the following pages).

Questions:

If what we learn in school is quickly outdated, how would education have to change over the next few years to ensure we don't fall hopelessly behind? And if our working lives eventually do stretch to 55 or 60 years, could people increasingly opt to start a second career halfway through their lives—which might require a second dose of education at a point in their lives when they probably haven't sat in a classroom for 25 years? What could be the impact on the institutions designing and delivering education? How much will be publicly owned and driven, as opposed to run by private enterprise?

MEET THE SPOUSES

What about marriage in a world of centenarians? Is it realistic to expect that someone who gets married in his or her 20s will stay with the same spouse for three-quarters of a century?

Divorce statistics sadly demonstrate that already today, a huge percentage of marriages don't even last 15 years, let alone 75. So the short answer to the question is, "Probably no." Could this mean that (like careers) everyone will have first, second, and third marriages?

Some will, for sure. But a number of trends are happening now that could have a significant cumulative impact on where marriage is heading as an institution. Increasing cohabitation, more children born out of wedlock, the rise of prenuptial agreements, the acceptance of same-sex marriages, and eventually, perhaps, socially sanctioned polygamy, could all bring about profound changes in marriage, family, and society.

Let's look at the trends. First, "living together without benefit of clergy" no longer carries any societal stigma. Depending on the country, between 10 and 30 percent of couples cohabit. The concept of marriage has already been knocked off its pedestal.

A huge percentage of children are born each year to unmarried parents—as high as 50 percent in Scandinavia. In the United Kingdom, about one family out of four with dependent children is headed by a single parent. In the United States, there are over 12 million such families, and merely lamenting this fact is frowned on as politically incorrect, regarded as a misguided attempt to impose middle-class values on people who are supposedly getting along just fine, thank you very much.

Traditional ideas about how a family should be structured have gone by the wayside.

Prenuptial agreements are also changing the game. Historically, one reason the concept of marriage developed in the first place was to preserve capital within the family being created. A prenup removes this economic justification for marriage, allowing the partners to pack up and leave with what they brought into the relationship, no questions asked. These agreements are not legally enforceable everywhere yet, but the idea is catching on. In one UK survey, 46 percent of all the respondents said they would want a prenuptial agreement with their spouse-to-be, in spite of the fact that they aren't legal there for the time being.

Admitting same-sex couples into the institution of marriage could prove to be a further step toward redefining what a family is. And the arrival in the West of more Muslim immigrants practicing polygamy could further break down resistance to the traditional idea that marriage must be between one man and one woman.

The cumulative impact of all these trends is that society could slowly scrap the idea of marriage itself as an old-fashioned relic from the past—quaint but completely unnecessary. While perhaps not completely displacing this fusty old tradition, a variety of alternative domestic arrangements, all contractually defined and legally protected as *civil unions*, could exist alongside it in ever greater numbers. Whether anybody calls these new arrangements "marriages" or not would be irrelevant: They would be de facto family units.

For example, if two men can marry and adopt children, thus forming a legal family, could a civil union eventually be deemed valid between two men and a woman? Or between three men and six women, for that matter? Once this barrier has been breached (and it could well be breached sometime in the next few years), unconventional communal arrangements could become very common, with adults joining by invitation, signing the papers, and becoming one of several wives or husbands in the newly extended union, or partnership—or "family," if you prefer.

Economically, such unions could be very strong, with several breadwinners, although it may not always be easy to make group decisions on how money is spent. On the other hand, maybe a seniority system could help decision making, just as in today's families: Mom's and/or Dad's vote always counts a bit more than the kids' votes.

Speaking of kids, raising children—the other historical reason why marriage developed—would become a communal responsibility. A civil union could even recruit new wives or mothers into the partnership specifically for that role. The resulting family units would be a hybrid between a kibbutz and the kind of matriarchal commune or "line marriage" that science fiction author Robert Heinlein brilliantly described in *The Moon Is a Harsh Mistress*, about life on a lunar colony.

Artificial families like this could be a real boon, allowing individuals, over a period of 70 or 80 years, to find the right fit within a group, then change to a new one if and when it makes sense for them to do so, rather than being stuck with the same spouse. . . for eight long decades.

Of course, this kind of arrangement wouldn't be for everybody. In the next decade, the vast majority of new families will probably come into being the old-fashioned way, through couples cohabiting or getting married. But a further breakdown of the perception of marriage as it has always been practiced seems to be in the cards.

Questions:

What could be the consequences for society if new kinds of unconventional family units take off? How could this change consumer attitudes and behavior? What business opportunities could it present? What new services and products might especially lend themselves to these new arrangements?

Redefining Education, One Screen at a Time

An industry that has changed very little in the past 150 years is education. How, when, and to whom education is delivered, and the building blocks of what we still call a basic education today, are ideas that were conceived during the Industrial Revolution and are still commonly used almost two centuries later. In fact, if you look only at the structure of the capstone institution of the education industry—the university—you'll even find leftover ideas not from the 1800s, but the *1400s*!

For many decades, if not centuries, education has been much the same animal, even if it has modernized in a few obvious respects. Think of the anachronism of a university laboratory outfitted with a million-dollar, state-of-the-art electron microscope, while the biology professor presiding over the lab enjoys a nineteenth-century employment perk called lifetime tenure and attends ceremonies wearing a medieval cap and gown. Tenure, by the way, is about professors pleasing their academic departments, not about pleasing their "consumers" (i.e., students). This is another way in which the university is out of synch with twenty-first-century reality.

Based on trends you can see around us right now, three key aspects of education—its cost, timing, and delivery—could change in the next decade. Since education affects literally everyone, big changes in the processes, economics, and intended outcomes of education could have a definite impact on our lives, especially on our children's lives. What's more, these changes could also have an impact on business, too, because they would potentially affect the quality and availability of talent. Your company's competitiveness, not to mention the competitiveness of an entire country, could depend on how education changes in the years ahead.

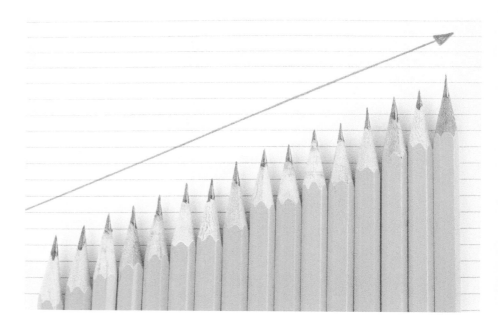

IT COSTS *HOW MUCH* TO GO TO COLLEGE?

Economically, a *bubble* forms when the price of some asset (e.g., tulip bulbs in Holland in the 1600s or houses in America from 1998 to 2006) inflates to an artificially and unsustainably high level—higher than the intrinsic value of the asset. Speculation is usually the driving force behind this run-up in prices, but a bubble can be made a lot worse if money is artificially injected into the market, making it even easier to buy that particular asset. For example, if the government subsidizes loans aimed at making the purchase possible, then even more buyers may pile into the market and drive prices spiraling higher and higher.

Is there a higher-education bubble building in America right now? Attending college was never cheap, but in the past 20 years, it has become more and more expensive. Since the late 1970s, college tuition in America has been skyrocketing at a rate about four times faster than the increase in the consumer price index. A school that charged $4,000 a year in tuition and fees a generation ago now costs more than $40,000 a year to attend.

How did this happen? The answer is simple: the Feds. In order to make a university education affordable to everyone (in theory a laudable goal) the US government lends money at preferential rates to students so they can buy a high-priced education. Channeled through these student loans, almost $100 billion in tax money is redistributed into the US education market each year.

Convinced they need a college education to get ahead ("It's the key to success!"), more students borrow more money, which inevitably results in price inflation. The schools simply raise their fees to soak up as much of this money as they can. Who can blame them? There's nothing to put any downward pressure on their tuition at all: no real price competition between schools, no regulatory bodies to keep prices in line. It's like a license to print money.

Some of these funds are put to excellent use, of course. Electron microscopes are not cheap, last time I looked. But the schools also spend a lot of the money they take in on bloated administrative staffs, expensive athletics programs, and, increasingly, on amenities such as luxury housing, gourmet dorm food, and climbing walls. These may help the schools from a marketing standpoint, but they don't add much to the quality of the actual education product.

Is the current trend sustainable? The recent economic downturn may be bringing this all to a halt—or at least to the point where some students and their parents are seriously rethinking the value of the education they should go into debt to pay for. Many new graduates leave school owing thousands of dollars to the federal government, yet they are unable to land a job that pays enough to allow them to pay off their debt. Suddenly, the return on investment (ROI) on their education is starting to look a lot different.

With certain degrees (e.g., engineering or computer sciences), graduates have a decent chance of landing a job that pays well. For them, the ROI on their education is acceptable, at least for the time being. However, if university fees continue to outpace salary growth, the ROI calculation even for fairly lucrative career paths will look worse and worse.

Not everyone goes to college to become an engineer or programmer, though. What if you want to major in nineteenth-century French literature, or to get a degree in some recently invented field such as cult film studies? Is it worthwhile to borrow heavily and spend perhaps $150,000 over four years (let's say four and a half years) only to end up with a degree that doesn't qualify you for work in a field paying a decent salary—or perhaps any field at all?

There's nothing wrong with getting a degree in basket weaving management or Latin American feminist studies. Then again, if it costs so much, is it economically intelligent? Far from liberating graduates to take wing in the grown-up world, a degree in a field with no marketability becomes a ball and chain that weighs them down instead. This realization is fueling the current protests on Wall Street, and could lead to a change in how higher education is priced, or paid for.

Questions:

Could students and their parents become more consumer-driven in their choice of higher education? Could price competition become a reality that universities would have to contend with? We should also remember that there's another factor at play here, too: demographics. The pool of young people (i.e., the prospective market for universities) is not growing, but rather *shrinking*. Faced with an ever-smaller number of 18-year-olds who are less and less willing to undertake the huge financial investment required, could tuition levels actually collapse? After all, that's the classic final phase of a bubble, when everyone bails out. If this happens, how would schools react? Would they cut back on their noncore activities? Would they emerge as different kinds of institutions than they are today? What might be the impact on the education offered?

THREE ALMA MATERS?

The next big change in education could have to do with the *timing* of its delivery. The way the industry's model works today, most of us are in the education pipeline from the time we're 5 until we're either 18 (high school), 22 (undergraduate university), or perhaps 25 or 26 (graduate school), give or take a year or so. This education is then supposed to last us the rest of our lives. Later in our lives, we may go on for some continuing education courses that last anywhere from a day or two to several weeks of seminars or courses that are usually work-related and paid for by our employer.

This model is becoming obsolete, fast. As mentioned earlier, our working lives are going to be longer, and could eventually span more than 60 years. Would people want to stay in a single career track that long? They may decide to fill those 60 years with three separate careers—for example a first, main career lasting 25 years (until about age 50), after which they embark on a second career for 10 or 15 more years, and finally another one taking them up to retirement at age 80 or even later. Another realistic scenario is that, along the way, they lose a job and decide to take advantage of the opportunity to make a career switch into something new.

Rapid obsolescence of what's taught in schools is, of course, another issue, as I've already mentioned. Taking these two points together, can an education, virtually all of which is delivered to you by the time you're 25, serve you until you're 80 or 90 years old?

Questions:

In the near future, could we receive not *an* education, but rather two or three educations? How might the first of these rounds of education (the one we get when we're still young) change ? What might a second or third education look like, assuming we partake of it while we are adults with other responsibilities? How much would it cost, and who would pay? How would society change if people made intensive forays back into the education pipeline as adults?

COMING SOON TO A SCREEN NEAR YOU

Distance learning is not new. Such well-known distance providers as Open University in the United Kingdom and the University of Phoenix in the United States offer accredited degrees that are delivered completely, or mostly, online. They have already been around for a few years and attract thousands of fee-paying students each year.

There's the rub: They still charge fees. However, you can take practically any Massachusetts Institute of Technology course online for free. One of the world's top universities, MIT decided in 2002 to put its courses, lecture notes, and educational materials on the Internet, available to anyone. The program is called MIT Open CourseWare (OCW).

Meanwhile, a virtual one-man-band of a university called the Khan Academy, operating since 2009, has created more than 2,600 video tutorials that are all available on YouTube. Covering a huge range of topics in math, science, economics, and finance, these 10-minute videos have generated almost 70 million views as of October 2011. And, of course, being on YouTube, they're free of charge as well.

MIT and the Khan Academy are pioneers. They also have funding for their ventures, which is obviously important if their content is to be offered without charging for it. MIT, for example, sinks $3.5 million a year into running OCW. Could other Khan Academies spring up over the next few years? If they do, the education industry may never be the same.

Why? Would these service providers spell the end of brick-and-mortar schools and universities? That's very doubtful. In the future, face-to-face learning will surely remain as important as ever, and schools will continue to provide this. But the flexible, quickly developing online programs could have a powerful influence on how teachers teach and how students learn—on the entire experience, from curriculum development and lesson planning to classroom discussion and interaction, even homework assignments.

For example, some teachers are already using Khan Academy tutorials to complement their own work, and they've established an innovative twist: The students watch the Khan tutorial (i.e., the lecture) on their own time at home, then do the "homework" exercises the next day in the classroom, with the teacher floating among them to give a helping hand where needed. In other words, the videos have flipped the conventional classroom experience on its head.

Questions:

Could public education head in this direction? Is there any reason why the tax money that funds public schools couldn't be used to develop a parallel Khan-like delivery system to complement in-class learning? How could that change the staffing and facilities at conventional schools?

Could Khan Academy–type tutorials make career switching easier? If gaining the necessary skill set for a new career doesn't entail huge costs in terms of money or time, could this new mode of delivery facilitate a trend toward three-career lives? Meanwhile, could online education pose a threat to the ability of brick-and-mortar schools to keep charging high tuition fees in the future? As more "education consumers" turn to these alternatives, could competition drive tuition fees lower at fee-charging universities? What happens to these schools when their revenue streams diminish?

Right now, a disadvantage of the Khan Academy–type alternative is that it isn't accredited and therefore can't offer an actual degree. How long will this remain the case? Or, perhaps a better question is, how long will this remain important? In the future, will knowledge trump credentials?

Web 9.0: How Will It Change Us?

In the past 15 years, the Internet has changed the world as dramatically as did gunpowder or movable type. But unlike these other two inventions, the Internet will continue to develop over the years, so the myriad changes it can potentially bring about are far from over.

How might the business landscape, our jobs, our lives, and—okay, let's be dramatic—the whole world be different a decade from now, thanks to the Web?

Even if it isn't easy for a tech nullity like myself to imagine all the things it may be able to do, it's worth reflecting about the future *consequences* of the Internet. Because what it will *do* is certainly intriguing, but perhaps even more interesting is what it could *do to us*. How might the Web continue to change the way we live and work?

SCHOOL? THERE'S AN APP FOR THAT

In a decade, most of the people on the planet could own handheld devices that give instantaneous access to 99.9 percent of the world's accu-

mulated knowledge. Actually, this device already exists, and you probably have one in your pocket right now. But future smartphones could be faster, cheaper, more user-friendly, and have an interface that facilitates the only tricky part of accessing all that information: asking the right questions.

Questions:

Can there be any doubt that handheld devices accessing the Web will also play a decisive role in the future of education? When every eight-year-old has such a smartphone, how could education change? Will we feel the need to teach things to children that everyone knows they could simply look up, anytime, anywhere? Do students need to know the content of the Constitution of the United States or that the Battle of Waterloo took place in 1815 when Wikipedia and a thousand other sites are accessible 24/7 on the gizmos they carry around (also 24/7)? Or could a large part of education center on teaching kids how to use this magnificent tool? It's a safe prediction that the Web (or rather, Web plus mobile device) will change education. But how could it change children—and childhood?

THE GLOBALIZATION OF EVERYTHING AND EVERYONE

It's not just big companies that move jobs offshore. Even at the individual level, the Internet allows us to globalize our networks, teams, and communities—to the possible detriment of local alternatives. I myself send work offshore to talented people I know in Austin, Zurich, and Belfast; for example, I collaborate online with a publisher in Maastricht, and my website 11changes.com was designed for me by developers in Mexico City whom I've never even met. I'm a one-man global conglomerate! You probably are, too.

Questions:

What impact could this trend have on your ability to create, compete, and react? Will far-flung dream teams take the place of equally capable people right here under your nose? Could the Web be helping you get the best talent in the world, yet also causing you to overlook talent just down the hall?

DISINTERMEDIATION OR MOTIVATION?

When was the last time you went to a travel agent to book a flight? When did you last walk into a bank and deal face-to-face with a teller? For that matter, when was the last time you went to a bookstore to buy a book? The Internet has enabled us to avail ourselves of a huge array of products and services directly, without much need for, or contact with, human intermediaries.

Cutting out the middle layer works in both directions, too: For example, while we consumers can go online to buy an MP3 version of a song, thus bypassing the music store, musicians can record songs and sell the MP3 to fans online, thus bypassing the record label. Both parties (consumers and producers) can develop strategies to use the Web to cut out the intermediaries they traditionally had to deal with.

Travel agents, bookstores, and bank tellers may all still exist in the physical world a decade from now, but if they do, could their roles need a rethink? In a world where people prefer to hop online and buy airline tickets or books directly, these people will need to add value—enough value that customers will be willing to pay more than they do online for the same product or service. Call the price difference a "human interface fee." How many people would be willing to pay this fee?

Questions:

Is the Web a fundamentally deflationary instrument, always steering buyers to the lowest prices and thus forcing prices down across the board? Or could this transparency prove to be the driving force behind a parallel development—namely, the flourishing of a service culture? If you're a seller and you know you don't offer the lowest price (which the Web can easily confirm), would you feel compelled to build up some other aspect of your offer so you would be competitive? Could this aspect be good old-fashioned human service?

PRIVACY: AN OUTDATED NOTION

Privacy is another concept that is being reshaped by the Internet. For example, here in Switzerland, Google Street View is required to obscure practically anything that could help to identify individuals inadvertently caught by its 360-degree cameras: not just faces and car license plate numbers, but even skin color and clothing. In Germany, residents can insist that Google blur images of their houses. Meanwhile, in Japan recently, a woman sued Google because her underwear was visible on Street View, hanging on a clothesline for all the world to see. (Sounds like a bunch of old fuddy-duddies to me.)

However, consider the other end of the spectrum. Teenagers seem only too happy to disclose an astonishing amount of information about themselves online. Instead of risks, they see benefits in sharing photos and personal information about themselves. Sharing helps them establish friendships and build communities.

Questions:

As Facebook-addicted Gen Yers grow older, could their idea of privacy (or rather, nonprivacy) become the norm in society? Could the value of being part of an open community be regarded as greater than the value of being sure that no one can see what your house (or underwear) looks like? Or, once they've grown up and acquired some assets worth protecting, could Gen Y revert to more conventional ideas about which information to share and which to keep private?

7 BILLION EYEWITNESSES

Imagine you're an evil dictator (it's easy if you try). One day a riot breaks out in the capital, and your troops start shooting protestors. When that happens, your regime's worst enemies are not the demonstrators but Twitter, Facebook, and YouTube. With their ability to zap eyewitness reports worldwide in seconds, these tools are very dangerous to you and your regime. They're perfect for stirring up reactions against you around the world, not to mention facilitating actual revolution by helping to direct and coordinate the mob in the streets.

Questions:

How might dictators fight back? Could they throw the switch and turn off the Internet? Could tweeting become a criminal act? Could the shock troops be ordered to go after anyone seen filming? More broadly, how could social media shape the future of political activism? If applying "Twitter pressure" to entrenched institutions can bring down authoritarian governments in Tunisia and Algeria, is it imaginable that their power could also help bring about the end of something much more benign——for example, the monarchy in the United Kingdom? What might have happened to Queen Elizabeth if Twitter had existed when Princess Diana died? Steered in just the right way, could social media bring people out on the streets to protest and fight. . . *anything?*

FACTS VERSUS OPINIONS

When I was growing up in the 1970s, my personal sources of information about what was going on in the world were the hometown newspaper, the CBS Evening News (God bless you, Walter Cronkite), a weekly flip through *Time* magazine, and the occasional three-minute news bulletin on the radio. At the time, these sources seemed to me to be utterly factual, utterly neutral, utterly trustworthy.

Today I get almost all my news online, and probably 80 percent of that is filtered through blogs. In other words, I'm often exposed to opinions about the news before I read the news itself. Sometimes I don't even have to get the facts; I'm more interested in the opinions about the facts.

Since the Web became interactive a few years ago, it's much more a medium of opinions than facts. (That's my opinion anyway.) Blogs, comments, flame wars, ratings, and reviews: The Web provides everyone a platform to opine, argue, hurl epithets, complain, urge, provoke, pontificate.

Where could this trend lead? Already, consumer reviews about a product are considered much more reliable than information published by the product's manufacturer. About half of all buyers consider opinions shared on their networks before making a purchase. According to one survey, 90 percent of consumers trust online recommendations from people they know—and 70 percent from people they don't know! In short, advice and opinions are sought out on the Web, and for the most part, they're trusted.

Questions:

When we all have the mobile devices I mentioned earlier, is it conceivable that a huge amount of our time will be spent accessing, digesting, and contributing to the ceaseless flow of opinions on the Web—recording our reactions to everything, documenting them with photos and videos, and dumping them into the maw of the Internet for the edification of our followers? Could there be an impact on business relationships? For example, could a hotel offer me a lower rate if I promise to post a positive review? Could I threaten to post a bad review unless I'm offered a discount? What happens to society when everyone has this power? Exposed to online opinions hundreds of times a day, might we learn to shut it all out and stop believing anything that anyone says about anything? How could this lack of trust change marketing, for example? Do we face a future of nothing but bitter cynicism and bad reviews?

FINDING MR. RIGHT

Depending on the source of the statistics, between 15 and 45 percent of newly married couples in the United States met online. In other countries, the figure appears to be between 5 and 10 percent, trending upward.

Questions:

What could be the consequences of this trend a decade from now? Could divorce rates be lower? After all, couples who meet online have already filled in the form, so to speak, and established their compatibility in a range of potentially touchy areas before even meeting for that first glass of chardonnay. They've vetted one another. Logically, this could mean that their marriages will be stronger.

Or could just the opposite be true? People are not logical; they're unpredictable. Sharing mutual interests is no guarantee that a relationship will last. If the thrill is gone, it's gone, even if you both adore Thai food, John Irving novels, and Earth, Wind & Fire. The Web makes it easier to look for a new partner. You could even be sifting through profiles online in the den while your spouse is in the living room watching TV. Could the Web therefore be a contributing factor to an *increase* in the divorce rate? By facilitating the possibility of moving on to greener pastures, could the Web turn us all into impatient perfectionists?

Food for thought!

POSTSCRIPT

THINKING THE UNTHINKABLE

> "Helping an organization visualize opportunities and threats that could materialize based on present trends, in order to improve its chances of future success."

That would not be a particularly sexy slogan for scenario planning, but it would be a fair description of the objectives of the technique.

The phrase "future success" can encompass many things, of course. If the organization in question is an entire country, then one "future success" its leaders should definitely want to achieve is ensuring the safety of its citizens. An important facet of that safety is preventing terrorist violence.

Especially following the attacks of September 11, 2001, security experts the world over would have been well advised to make use of scenario thinking in order to map out the potential "threat landscapes" in which their countries might find themselves. Such a process could help them identify the vulnerabilities—physical, legal, and even psychological—that would emerge as various geopolitical currents were taking shape during the decade past, as public attitudes toward security were coming into focus, as national policies were being implemented that might put a country in terrorists' crosshairs, and as actual acts of terror were taking place across the globe that could be studied and analyzed.

Then in the summer of 2011 came a massacre in Norway. Immediately following this horrific event, I couldn't shake the impression that the security forces there had probably never conducted such an exercise. Otherwise, it would have been more apparent that Norwegian policymakers, for all their peaceable good intentions, understood their country was not immune to terrorist violence. Had they acknowledged this as a real possibility, they might have thought through their antiterror procedures and beefed up relevant capabilities—just in case.

After all, a number of factors following 9/11 could have given Norwegian security forces good reason to believe the country could one day become an al-Qaeda target. For example, Norway's participation as a NATO member in the military campaign in Afghanistan or its minor role in the Muhammad cartoons scandal could antagonize jihadists. Merely as a rich, secular Western society, it qualified as a potential target.

As it happened, al-Qaeda wasn't the perpetrator of the terror attack in Oslo and Utøya. But that's beside the point; what is more important is that Norway seemed completely unprepared for any such attack from any direction whatsoever—not only in terms of its lax security, but especially in its overconfident, even relaxed, mind-set, which was ultimately accountable for the magnitude of the disaster. Even after terrorists had struck targets in the United States, Madrid, Bali, London, Moscow, Mumbai, and several other places, Norwegians seemed to dismiss the very possibility that anyone might ever want to do them harm. As a consequence of this head-in-the-sand mentality, many preventive measures—obvious in hindsight—were not taken, perhaps not even deemed necessary. The following were merely the most glaring oversights:

- No effective security detail existed, either on the island or in the form of an offshore patrol by the Norwegian Coast Guard, for a gathering of several hundred teenagers considered VIPs by the country's ruling political party. Any way you look at it, this was a high-value, very vulnerable target.

- No thought was given to the possible need to have boats at the ready in case the island might need to be evacuated or people onshore might need to get to the island quickly.

- No helicopter pilots were available for the police's special SWAT unit (they were all on vacation), and apparently no thought was given to improvising on the spot—for example, by commandeering one of the helicopters being used by TV crews filming the carnage.

- There was no difficulty driving a car packed with explosives into the heart of the city's government district and parking it unattended outside the building housing the prime minister's office.

- No system existed for reporting to authorities the possibly suspicious purchase by a "farmer" of several tons of fertilizer, which, from previous tragic experience, was well known as a potential ingredient in concocting homemade explosives.

- There was no surveillance or systematic collection of intelligence on extremist political activity, online or offline, especially the capability of connecting the dots with other potentially alarming information, such as the fact that an extremist was buying bomb-making materials.

- There was no ability to track the purchase or acquisition of automatic weapons, not to mention the purchase of enough ammunition to fuel a murderous shooting rampage lasting 90 minutes.

It's always easy to criticize others' mistakes, especially in hindsight, and that's not my intention here. Rather, I'd like to pose this question: The proximal cause for the tragedy that day may have come down to ineffective police action and bad luck, but underneath it all, wasn't the real problem a failure of imagination on the part of the people with the responsibility to keep their compatriots safe? What may have doomed all those youngsters was an inability, or worse, unwillingness by Norwegians to imagine scenarios that might seem completely contrary to the way they perceived themselves but that were nonetheless possible. Never having given serious consideration to such scenarios, painful as the process might have been, meant they were caught off guard when an attack actually materialized. The massacre was a strategic planning failure as much as anything else.

Scenario thinking might not have prevented the terrorism in Oslo and Utøya, but if the politicians, police officers, and other authorities responsible for security had developed an array of possible terror scenarios, it's at least imaginable that security might have been tighter and the police better prepared and quicker to react. And that could have saved some of the young lives lost on that terrible summer day.

“Chance favors the **prepared** mind.”

Louis Pasteur

Photo credits

Images used throughout this book are either from the author's personal collection or are copyrighted images from iStockPhoto that have been used with permission. Exceptions include the following:

Introduction: Albert Einstein. ©Corbis/Spector. Used with permission.
Chapter 4: *The Scream* by Edvard Munch. ©Corbis/Spector. Used with permission.
Chapter 4: Archduke Franz Ferdinand and Sophie Leaving Sarajevo Senate. ©Corbis/Spector. Used with permission.
Postscript: Photo ©Adrian Øhrn Johansen. Used with permission.